BERLITZ®

Euro Disney Resort

By the staff of Berlitz Guides

2nd Edition (1992/1993)

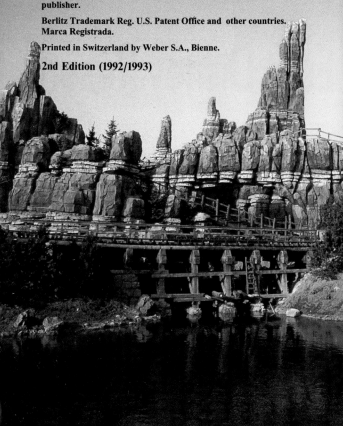

How to use this guide

- All the practical information, hints and tips that you will need before and during the trip start on p. 105.
- For general background, see Euro Disney Resort: the Lands and the Characters, p. 6, and A Brief History, p. 16.
- The sights are described on pp. 30–73.
- ✓ Our own choice of sights most highly recommended is pinpointed by the Berlitz symbol.
- For hotel and restaurant information, see pp. 85–95.
- Shopping, sports, entertainment and nightlife are described f r o m pp. 74–85.
- If there's anything you can't find, refer to the index, pp. 126–8.

Although we have made every effort to ensure the accuracy of all the information in this book, changes occur incessantly. We cannot therefore take responsibility for any facts, prices, addresses and circumstances in general that are constantly subject to alteration.

Text: Jack Altman
Berlitz copyright photos: Claude Huber
Cartography: Visual Image

We should like to thank Wendy Wolfe, Lorie Lichtlen, Isabelle Vartanian and all the other members of the enormously helpful Euro Disney staff for their co-operation in the preparation of this book.

CONTENTS

Cover picture: © THE WALT DISNEY COMPANY

5

Euro Disney Resort: the Lands and the Characters

America's most popular ambassador, Mickey Mouse, has set up a huge holiday home and playground just outside Paris: the Euro Disney Resort. He, his wife Minnie and pals Goofy, Pluto and Donald Duck are the hosts of Europe's biggest theme park, and plenty more besides.

The Euro Disney Resort merits much more than just a day trip. It offers a comprehensive holiday centre with multiple attractions and facilities for a stay of several days. The first part of the resort covers some 600 hectares (nearly 1,500 acres) and there are ambitious plans for future expansion. Besides the theme park, there's an artificial lake, entertainment centre, a championship-size golf course, tennis courts, swimming pools, luxury and moderately priced hotels, camping facilities, restaurants and a convention centre.

The resort is located at Marne-la-Vallée, 32 km (20 miles) east of Paris. A new motorway (*auto-route*) provides easy access both from the capital and from the international airports of Roissy (Charles de Gaulle) and Orly. Rapid commuter trains (RER) from Paris and (from 1994) high-speed long-distance trains (TGV) from the provinces drop visitors

Walt Disney wanted to create 'the happiest place on earth'.

off near the entrance to the theme park: Euro Disneyland.

The Theme Park

Euro Disneyland, like all the creations inspired by Walt Disney's fertile imagination, is the stuff that dreams are made of. Those dreams have their roots in the old world of Europe, the New World of Main Street America and the Wild West, and the timeless worlds of outer space. From France come the tales of Sleeping Beauty and Cinderella as told by Charles Perrault; from Britain,

James Barrie's Peter Pan and Lewis Carroll's Alice; from Germany, Snow White and the Seven Dwarfs as told by the brothers Grimm; from Italy, Carlo Collodi's Pinocchio.

The theme park is divided up into five 'lands' – Frontierland, Adventureland, Fantasyland and Discoveryland – all leading off from Main Street, USA, a land all to itself.

Recapturing the traditions of small-town America, Main Street is the starting point for the park's activities. Here you will see the candy shops and ice-cream parlours of America's 20th-century childhood. At the barber shop, Dad can get an old-fashioned shave and short-back-and-sides haircut, while the rest of the family is serenaded by a quartet of crooners. A Statue of Liberty tableau is a reminder that the New York monument was a gift from France, host nation to Euro Disneyland, in the 1880s.

The dream voyage into past and future really gets into gear with the tour of the four 'lands' bordering on Main Street. Frontierland captures the pioneering atmosphere of an American mining town and the Wild West, complete with ranch, shooting gallery and Indian canoes. Steam-powered paddle-boats cruise on the river. Thrill-seekers should head for the soaring, plunging Big Thunder Mountain attraction, or scare themselves stiff among the 999 ghosts of gold prospectors in Phantom Manor.

The big attraction at Adventureland is a sail on the high seas with the Pirates of the Caribbean. On Adventure Isle you can explore caves, tunnels and waterfalls. Children can also climb up

Careful attention to detail makes Main Street buildings special.

into the tree-top house of the Swiss Family Robinson.

Fantasyland draws more directly on the fun of Walt Disney's classic animated films. The major focus – indeed the symbol of Euro Disneyland itself – is Sleeping Beauty's towering castle, officially known by its French name, Le Château de la Belle au Bois Dormant. Other attractions include a ride with Pinocchio; the cottage where Snow White lives with the Seven Dwarfs; losing yourself in the maze of Alice in Wonderland; and flying away with Peter Pan or Dumbo the elephant.

From the fairy-tale past of Fantasyland, Discoveryland whisks you back to the present and beyond it to the future. Benefiting from the advanced electronics developed at Walt Disney Imagineering, you can ride in a spaceship at Star Tours, an ultra-modern sports car at Autopia, or join Michael Jackson as 'Captain EO' in a 3-D movie at CinéMagique. Le Visionarium presents an escapade with adventure-writer Jules Verne on a 360° screen.

Everywhere you go you see hosts Mickey, Minnie, Goofy, Donald Duck and Pluto wandering around in their familiar costumes, happy to pose with visitors for souvenir photographs. They and other Disney characters are the stars of the great night-time illuminated parade down Main Street, USA.

At the End of the Ride
At every turn, you realize that this is much, much more than a simple amusement park. Restaurants go far beyond the usual hamburger and hot-dog outlets, though there are those as well. On Main Street you will find traditional American establishments, from coffee-shop to old-fashioned diner. Frontierland serves steaks, barbecues and Tex-Mex food, while Adventureland offers spicy kebabs and Caribbean-style seafood. In Fantasyland there is everything from pizza to gourmet seafood, and in Discoveryland, 9

naturally enough, is the fastest food the cosmos have ever imagined.

There is music galore – brass bands, Dixieland jazz, Wild West cancan dancing in Frontierland, a mini-musical comedy at Le Château de la Belle au Bois Dormant (Sleeping Beauty's Castle), rock 'n' roll at Videopolis, a Caribbean steel band in Adventureland – plus entertainment from conjurors, acrobats and slapstick comedians.

Disney's own accommodation immediately surrounding the theme park includes two luxury, two first-class and two moderately priced hotels, plus extensive camping grounds for caravans and tents.

For sports enthusiasts there are tennis courts, swimming pools, health clubs and an 18-hole golf course (with nine more holes to be added in 1993).

The Euro Disney Resort is within easy reach of all the sights of Paris, the châteaux of Versailles, Fontainebleau and Vaux-le-Vicomte, the Champagne vineyards and the nearby royal city of Reims. A visit to the Euro Disney Resort and the surrounding towns and countryside is a total holiday.

Mickey Mouse and his Pals

The little creatures leaping around the dreamland of Walt Disney's imagination have become icons of the 20th century. The mice and ducks and dogs have each taken on a distinct character, conjured up by the Disney cartoons and comic strips in inimitable fashion. Here is a portrait gallery of Mickey and the chief members of his gang.

Mickey Mouse, said the great Russian film director Sergei Eisenstein, has been 'America's most original contribution to culture'. He made a rather brutal screen début in 1928 as the helmsman in *Steamboat Willie*. Mickey terrorized the animals aboard the boat to make music for his orchestra, twanging a cat's tail, hammering xylophone-style on a cow's teeth, kicking piglets away at feeding time so that he could tweak the sow's teats. Thereafter, Walt's hero – 'I love Mickey Mouse,' he once said, 'more than any woman I've known' – became strictly Mr Nice Guy.

His adventures showed him to be courageous, impudent but never again nasty, cheerful, persevering, loving and loyal. If ever Mickey strayed from the all-American ideal, the Disney studios would receive indignant letters of protest from fans and citizens' groups.

Walt Disney himself provided the best physical description of Mickey Mouse: 'His head was a

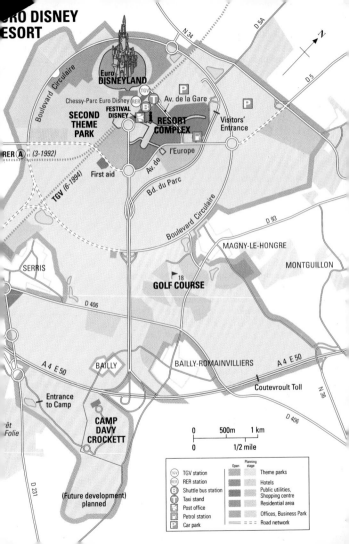

Mickey welcomes his Steamboat Willie *self across the decades to Disneyland.*

circle with an oblong circle for a snout. The ears were circles so they could be drawn the same no matter how he turned his head. His body was like a pear and he had a long tail. His legs were pipestems and we stuck them in big shoes to give him the look of a kid wearing his father's shoes.' Why gloves? 'More human.' Why not five fingers? 'Too much on such a little figure, so we took one away. That was just one less finger to animate.'

Those famous Mickey Mouse ears were so endearing that in World War II they were put on children's gas masks to make these fearsome objects more acceptable.

Minnie Mouse is officially Mickey's wife, after appearing for years as the heroine for whose hand in marriage he had to go through fire and water over and over again. However, you never actually see her marry him. Walt Disney declared that though 'in private life' she was Mickey's wife, 'Minnie is, for screen purposes, his leading lady.' In early roles she resists his advances, slapping his face when he gets too 'fresh'. Later, she demurely waits for him to get through his adventures to win her.

Her costume is usually distinguished by an oversize ribbon in her hair or a hat with a long-

Of all the cartoon characters Disney created, Mickey Mouse remained his favourite.

stemmed flower and a rather saucy glimpse of frilly white panties beneath her skirt.

The august British novelist E.M. Forster provided a fine character sketch: 'She appears to be of independent means and to own a small house in the midst of unattractive scenery, where, with no servants and little furniture, she busies herself with trifles until Mickey comes. Without him, her character shines not. As he enters, she expands, she becomes simple, tender, brave and strong, and her coquetterie is of the delightful type which never conceals its object. Ah, that squeak of greeting! As you will have guessed from it, her only fault is hysteria.'

Donald Duck came on the scene six years after Mickey and rather surprised Walt by ousting the mouse as the major star of the Disney studio. If Mickey has remained the company's unchallenged emblem and the founder's personal favourite, the insufferable Donald has asserted himself as the most popular of all the Disney cartoon characters. (He has appeared in 128 movies compared with Mickey's 77.)

With Mickey safely cast as the good guy, Donald could give full vent to his preposterous rages, non-stop mischief and a cocky pride perpetually suffering **13**

self-inflicted injury. Conscious of the restraints imposed on Mickey by America's high moral expectations of him, a writer at the Disney studio noted that Donald 'was our outlet. We could use all the ideas for him we couldn't use on Mickey. Donald became our ham, a mean, irascible little buzzard. Everyone knew he was bad and didn't give a damn'.

What makes the Duck's unabashed malice palatable is his equally indomitable courage against all odds – and the fact that he always gets his comeuppance. In his delightfully silly little sailor suit, his repartee is superb, not least because, although it is carefully scripted, you can never understand a word he says.

In the 1970s politicians in Chile accused Donald very seriously of being a CIA agent. Nobody has ever found evidence to disprove this – or prove it!

Pluto, like Mickey, made a fierce début before mellowing to become a faithful, tender-hearted household companion. In *The Chain Gang* (1930) Pluto was one of a pair of vicious-looking bloodhounds hunting down escaped prisoner Mickey. By the next film, Mickey had tamed him into using his tail as a windscreen wiper for the car. Pluto's docile good nature makes him a sucker for Donald's callous tricks. The only time he himself gets mean is when there is a cat around. His love life has been quite uneventful, staying faithful to Fifi, who bore him five pups, though he did have a brief fling with a highly sophisticated dachshund named Dinah.

Goofy lives up to his name. His trademarks are his laugh – an utterly ridiculous guffaw – and two very widely set front teeth. His appeal derives from an ability to raise his natural stupidity to the level of high art. The key moment in his adventures is when his latest act of foolishness suddenly dawns on him, heralded by the beginning of the slowest smile in the Western world. Unlike Pluto, who rarely wears anything but a collar, this dog likes overalls or rolled-up jeans and a floppy waistcoat. The natural enemies of this good-hearted bumbler – too chaotic to be a household pet – are not cats, rats or other small creatures, but everyday inanimate objects – furniture, car engines, pianos, all likely to turn ferocious in his presence. His studio creator, Art Babbitt, described him as 'the kind of character that thought very hard and very long about everything he did. And then he did it wrong'.

Mickey and Minnie pose for their fans.

15

A Brief History

Serious plans to create a Disneyland in Europe first emerged in 1975, nine years after Walt Disney's death, but Walt had already been contemplating building Disney-style theme parks back in the 1930s. When the parks did become a reality, from 1955 on, their immediate success was in large part due to Disney's simple idea of building them with the same meticulous care that his studio brought to a full-length feature film. He drew on the talents of the studio's animators, set designers, directors and writers to develop the park's attractions. To understand Euro Disneyland, the latest of the Disney theme parks, follow the story of Walt Disney himself.

In the Beginning

Like so many of America's true originals – those that captured the unifying spirit of a people in their complex diversity – Disney grew up in the nation's heartland, the Middle West. Walter Elias Disney was born in a small wood-frame house in Chicago on 5 December 1901. His father was a Canadian-born building contractor of Anglo-Irish descent, his mother came from Ohio. His family – which included a sister, Ruth, and three brothers, Herbert, Raymond and Roy – moved to a farm in Missouri when Walt was a small child. He worked on the land, and conceived no special love for animals (he later confessed to a lifelong fear of, yes, that ferocious beast, the mouse), but he did do his first drawings in the farmyard.

After the Disneys moved on to Kansas City, Walt took his first art lessons at the age of 14, at the local art institute. Two years later, he was in Chicago again, and received help from a newspaper cartoonist, Leroy Gossett.

In 1919, just too late for battle action in World War I, Walt became an ambulance driver for the US Army in France, at Neufchâteau in Alsace. His artwork there was limited to decorating his ambulance with caricatures and painting fake medals on his buddies' leather jackets. A letter to his high-school friends began, 'Bonjour comrades, France is an interesting place but just the same I want to go home to my Mama.' He illustrated the letter with some jolly cartoons of 'Boche prisoners captured by the Americans'.

Walt's career in animated cartoons began in earnest back in

Walt may not have drawn Mickey Mouse himself, but he created his inimitable personality.

Kansas City. There he teamed up with artist Ubbe 'Ub' Iwerks to produce commercials for local cinemas, topical 'Laugh-o-Grams', and updated fairy tales based on Cinderella, Little Red Riding Hood and Puss in Boots.

Walt and Mickey Come to Hollywood

The company's most ambitious series, entitled *Alice's Wonderland*, artfully combined animated cartoons and live action, but the costs broke the studio. In 1923, with $40 and the reels of *Alice's Wonderland* in his bags, Walt took off for Los Angeles. He rented an office and worked on a new set of *Alice Comedies*.

Disney was determined to transform animated cartoons from what the Hollywood industry had always regarded as an amusing sideline into a full-scale commercial enterprise. He brought Iwerks out to streamline the artwork, while he concentrated on the production side. His brother Roy, seven years older, provided the solid business sense. By his own admission never a great draughtsman, Walt abandoned the drawing board in 1926, preferring to conceive and develop ideas, then realize them

through the best professionals he could find.

In 1927 Disney switched from live-action films to full animation for his *Oswald the Lucky Rabbit* series. The wide-eyed, round-bodied hero was an unmistakable graphic precursor of Mickey Mouse. When he lost the rights to the Oswald character in a contractual dispute with a distributor in New York, Disney learnt a valuable lesson. Never again would a single aspect of Walt Disney's enterprises – from the reproduction of films on video down to the lowliest T-shirt or pencil bearing the likeness of a Disney character – escape the protection of watertight copyright. According to the legend Walt himself liked to perpetuate, it was on the train back from New York to Los Angeles that he conceived the idea of Mickey Mouse.

The actual moment of creation is veiled in mystery, but it does seem that Walt's own choice of name for the mouse was Mortimer, until his wife, Lillian, dismissed it as ridiculous and proposed Mickey. Significantly, a mouse named Mortimer turned up a few years later, given short shrift when wooing Minnie in *Mickey's Rival*. In any case, we do know that the actual drawing of Mickey was executed by Ub Iwerks, though it was Walt who **18** chose his wardrobe – velvet trousers with two huge pearl buttons, plus a pair of four-fingered gloves and big, round-toed shoes.

Of course, nobody disputes the fact that Walt Disney conceived Mickey's personality (see p.10). The mouse epitomized the Disney philosophy in a world of uncomplicated values where right is right and wrong is wrong.

Mickey's great stroke of luck was that he arrived in Hollywood at the same time as sound pictures. In 1928, a year after Al Jolson had caused a sensation in *The Jazz Singer*, Mickey Mouse starred in the first synchronized sound cartoon, *Steamboat Willie*. (Two earlier, silent Mickey films, *Plane Crazy* and *Gallopin' Goucho*, had been held up so they could be released later in sound form.) In the same landmark film, Minnie Mouse also came aboard – literally, when Mickey was manning the helm of the steamboat and yanked her on deck from the river bank with a boathook caught in her panties.

Rise to Greatness

With people in the depressed 1930s eager for some fun, Mickey rapidly achieved international fame (he was renamed Topolino in Italy and Miki Kuchi in Japan) both in film and comic-book form. Mickey's faithful dog Pluto turned up as a simple-minded bloodhound in *The Chain*

Gang. The chronically incompetent Goofy appeared first in *Mickey's Revue* (1932) and, renamed Dingo, won the hearts of the French, with the same kind of appeal they were later to discern in Jerry Lewis. The *Silly Symphony* series offered ingenious interaction of music and animation technique in the first colour films, most notably in *King Neptune* and *Babes in the Wood*.

The great event of 1934 was the arrival of Donald Duck. His début in *Wise Little Hen* as an impossibly bad-tempered troublemaker immediately challenged the popularity of Mickey himself.

Branching out beyond films, the Disney company started on the road that was to lead to the Disneyland theme parks. In the 1930s Santa Barbara, California, saw the first Saturday morning Mickey Mouse Clubs with the marching bands, songs and dances that have become a staple of the entertainment on the parks' Main Street, USA. Mickey Mouse writing pads had been produced as early as 1929, but serious merchandising, a major feature of the parks, got underway in 1935 with Disney-decorated jewellery, spoons, mugs, teapots, dolls, plates, hairbrushes and biscuits. The Ingersoll company was saved from bankruptcy when it was licensed to sell the famous Mickey Mouse wristwatch – and

Walt's Secret
At the core of Disney's genius was his perfectionism. He watched over the tiniest detail, often driving collaborators crazy with demands to get every button, every toenail just right. He was obsessed by his work and could not understand people who did not share his obsession. But it was what distinguished the quality of the Disney studio's work and enabled it to command worldwide attention while other animation studios simply provided almost anonymous filler material.

When the day came to create the first Disneyland theme park, the same tireless professionalism and meticulous concern for detail prevented it becoming just another amusement park. Disney was almost excessively proud of sharing the ordinary tastes of the ordinary guy and going to extraordinary lengths to display them.

sold 2,000,000 in the first eight weeks.

Even within the realm of cinema, *Music Land* (1935) had the look of a theme park. From the *Silly Symphony* series, it tells the Romeo-and-Juliet-style love story of the king's son from the Isle of Jazz wooing the enemy queen's daughter from the Land of Symphony. The Isle of Jazz is a warm kingdom of brassy horns, honky-tonks and saxophone skyscrapers, while the Land of Symphony has the cool opulence of a European château, complete with towering organ and a metronome-shaped lookout post. The happy ending of double weddings uniting the kingdoms on the Bridge of Harmony has all the makings of a Disneyland parade.

Even the film studio was conceived with all the neatness of future Disneylands. Janet Flanner, who became famous as the *New Yorker* magazine's Paris correspondent, wrote in 1936: 'The studio looks like a small municipal kindergarten with green grass for the children to keep off of and, on the roof, a gigantic glorious figure of Mickey to show them the best way.'

Snow White Meets the Dwarfs and Donald Goes to War

The one stone that was lacking in the Disney edifice to make it a fully fledged equal of the major studios such as MGM or Warner Bros was, quite simply, a full-length feature film. The breakthrough came with *Snow White and the Seven Dwarfs* (1937). For it, Disney hired 300 new artists.

The animation for an 83-minute film was infinitely more complex than for cartoon shorts. The smoother movements of

human figures – Snow White, the Dwarfs, Prince and Wicked Queen – required much more sophisticated drawings than had been used for the stylized animal characters of Mickey and his gang. A new multiplane camera was introduced to provide depth of field for an illusion of perspective and to handle broader areas of action covered by increased numbers of figures.

The graphic tone was set by Swiss-born Albert Hurter, who had earlier given *Music Land* and *Three Little Pigs* a more distinctively European touch with images from the Gothic fairy tales of his childhood.

Unlike any cartoon film before it, but just like any grand new movie 'event', *Snow White and the Seven Dwarfs* was given a glamourous gala première in Hollywood, with Marlene Dietrich, Charles Laughton and Judy Garland in the audience. It was an instant box-office hit and won a special Academy Award, a big Oscar for Snow White and seven little ones for the Dwarfs.

Produced in the new studios at Burbank, the next full-length feature, *Pinocchio*, was acclaimed by critics as a masterpiece. It made a perfect marriage of artistry and dazzling technique with a timeless fairy tale. However, released in the menacing days of 1940, the poignant story of how woodcarver Geppetto's boy-puppet comes alive was perhaps too sombre to match the spectacular commercial success of *Snow White*.

The Disney studio continued to extend the boundaries of its cinematic technique with *Fantasia* (also 1940). It invented animated visualizations of classical music by Bach, Beethoven, Tchaikovsky, Stravinsky and, most memorably, Paul Dukas' *The Sorcerer's Apprentice*. The latter episode gave Mickey Mouse his chance to make a starring comeback against the recent pushy triumphs of Donald Duck. He is both hilarious and disturbing as the apprentice overwhelmed by magic spells that seem to let him play with the whole universe.

Two lighter features – *Dumbo*, the elephant who learns to fly, and the forest adventures of the deer, *Bambi* – were released in 1941 and 1942, just before Disney, along with the rest of America, went to war. The studios were commandeered to billet an anti-aircraft unit and to make animation films for training the US Armed Forces. Donald Duck

In Snow White *the animator's art reached a new peak of sophistication.*

Pinocchio discovers that telling lies won't get him out of gaol.

proved to be Disney's most effective weapon when it came to boosting morale both at home and on the battle front. With the official blessing of Disney's copyright lawyers, GIs were issued with military insignia caricatures of Commando Donald. The Duck's cartoon, *Der Fuehrer's Face,* had everyone rolling in the aisles at his nightmare of working in a Nazi German munitions factory before waking up to pelt Hitler's portrait with tomatoes.

The Road to Disneyland

After World War II Disney continued to produce cartoon features that were to provide many of his future theme parks' most popular characters, among them *Cinderella* (1950), *Alice in Wonderland* (1951) and *Peter Pan* (1953). A modified version of the castle in *Sleeping Beauty*

(1959) has now become the centrepiece of the Euro Disney Resort.

A 1946 feature, *Song of the South*, combined live and animated action, and Disney turned increasingly to making live-action films, such as Robert Louis Stevenson's *Treasure Island* (1949) and the Jules Verne classic *20,000 Leagues Under the Sea* (1954), starring James Mason and Kirk Douglas. Both of these included adventures that inspired key attractions in the theme parks. *Swiss Family Robinson* (1960) was not a great commercial success, but the family's tree house has turned out to be a favourite theme park crowd-puller.

The creation of the first Disneyland theme park became Walt Disney's major preoccupation. It grew out of doctors' advice to the chronic workaholic to relax from the stress of studio work. Like many adults of his generation, Walt loved model trains. He was particularly taken with the work of two of his animators, Ollie Johnston and Ward Kimball, who were building their own steam engine and backyard railway. In 1947 Walt followed suit on a big scale. He had tracks laid around his home, complete with a small-scale engine, cattle-cars and box-cars, with a tunnel going under his wife's flower garden. As the thing expanded, he wanted to run it around the Burbank studios. There was no room, so he incorporated the idea into an old dream of his, a Disney-style amusement park.

Back in the 1930s he had been disappointed by the lack of inventiveness in the ordinary playgrounds and amusement parks to which he took his daughters, Diane and Sharon. His desire to launch his own version there and then was curbed by investment in the new Burbank studio and the outbreak of World War II. In 1952 he set up a company named WED (Walter Elias Disney) to plan the park with a team of designers from the studio's animation department. For the site, he bought 160 acres (65 hectares) of orange groves in Anaheim, on the southern outskirts of Los Angeles. The name: Disneyland.

In it, like the woodcarver Geppetto with Pinocchio, Walt Disney could bring his dream to life. At last he had a place big enough to set up his railway. It would define the park's perimeter. Disneyland would represent the America of Walt's own childhood and his already legendary films. The railway's main station was set at the entrance to Main Street, USA. The street would take visitors through an old-fashioned, slightly smaller than lifesize replica of a small, typically American downtown area – city hall, fire station, shops and drugstore, trams and horse-drawn streetcars. At Main Street's far end was Sleeping Beauty's Castle, the chief attraction, from which a clockwise route would take visitors to Adventureland, Frontierland, Fantasyland and Tomorrowland.

These lands were peopled with characters from Disney's films and animated by their adventures. Disneyland was designed like an elaborate film studio, built with the same skills, and by the same people, that are used to make film sets, with the park's entertainments, shops and restaurants operating behind glorious décors. Like watching a film, a visit to the park would follow a sequence of 'events', with the designers' pre-planned scenic changes – but this time in an order chosen by the visitor. When the first Disneyland attractions were created, Walt himself would be on site with a stopwatch in hand to time to the second the proper length of each 'ride'. At Euro Disneyland, each ride has been stopwatched with the same precision.

On 17 July 1955 Disneyland was opened for 30,000 guests. The inauguration was broadcast live on television, offering unprecedented publicity for a 'mere' amusement park. Over 4,000,000 visitors attended in the first year, and the number

Walt Disney's passion for railways greatly influenced the theme parks' character.

24

increased to 10,000,000 once it got into its stride.

The secret of its triumph over other amusement parks seemed to lie in Disney's ability to appeal not only to children but also to the child in every adult. It was not always clear whether children were begging their parents to take them to Disneyland or vice versa. In a speech to Hollywood executives in 1959, Soviet leader Nikita Khrushchev railed at the US State Department for invoking 'security reasons' to keep him away from Disneyland.

From Disneyland to Euro Disney Resort

Walt Disney died of lung cancer on 16 December 1966, but not before scouting a location in Florida for a bigger, even more ambitious theme park. Walt Disney World Resort, as it became known, opened its Magic Kingdom in Orlando, Florida, in 1971, soon followed by EPCOT (Experimental Prototype Community Of Tomorrow). On land covering 27,443 acres (11,110 hectares) – twice the size of Manhattan Island – the company was this time able to build its own hotels and service areas and pre-empt the uncontrolled construction that had quickly surrounded the Disneyland site at Anaheim.

Both WDW's Magic Kingdom and EPCOT drew on the very latest electronic and laser technology to update the attractions. Techniques first tried out for a lifelike robot of President Abraham Lincoln in 1964 were used by Disney's so-called 'Imagineers' to create '*Audio-Animatronics*', a patented system of automated figures to people the Haunted Mansion and Pirates of the Caribbean, two attractions also featured at Euro Disneyland.

In 1983 Tokyo Disneyland opened on 600 acres (243 hectares) of reclaimed land in Tokyo Bay. Within a year it equalled the California Disneyland figure of nearly 10,000,000 visitors a year.

The adventure starts at Main Street Station for Euro Disneyland visitors.

Under the new company chairman, Michael Eisner, previously a top executive at Paramount, the theme parks tightened their traditional tie-in with the film industry. *Star Wars* director George Lucas, who as a child had attended the opening of Disneyland in 1955, was brought in to work with 'Imagineers' on a new outer space ride named *Star Tours*. Celebrated for films such as *The Godfather* and *Apocalypse Now*, Francis Ford Coppola directed an extravagant science-fiction spec-

tacle starring rock star Michael Jackson, to be screened in the new Cinémagique hall. Both of these are featured at Euro Disneyland.

Eisner also opened the Disney–MGM Studios Theme Park in Florida in 1989. It takes visitors through the history and all the make-believe, mysteries and technical wizardry of film making as created by two of Hollywood's most famous studios. A similar park is to be opened next to Euro Disneyland in 1995.

The idea for a European Disney theme park first emerged in the mid 1970s. Britain, Italy, Spain and France were all at one time considered possible sites. Britain and Italy quickly lost out because they lacked an appropriate expanse of available flat land. The site located in Spain's Alicante had a desirable Florida-like climate most of the year but was also bedevilled by gusty mistral winds.

In the end, the French site of Marne-la-Vallée was chosen for its proximity to Paris and central

Michael Eisner, Roy Disney and Robert Fitzpatrick at the inauguration of the Euro Disney Resort.

position for western Europe. This gave it very good demographics – 68 million people living within a four-hour drive and 300 million within a two-hour flight. There was no need to go to the lengths taken in rainy Tokyo and roof over all of Main Street: uncertainties in the French climate and inclement winters would be offset by a series of covered arcades, protected waiting areas and such innovations as redesigned coaches for the Euro Disneyland Railroad.

In December 1985 Michael Eisner signed a first letter of agreement with the French Socialist government of Laurent Fabius and drew up the financial contract with the Conservative government of Jacques Chirac the following spring. Under the direction of Euro Disney president Robert Fitzpatrick, a leading organizer at the Los Angeles Olympics of 1984, Euro Disneyland was completed for opening on 12 April 1992. The executives and politicians gave way to Walt Disney's old buddies, Mickey, Minnie, Donald, Pluto and Goofy, to welcome in the crowds.

Disney characters wait to welcome the crowds at Euro Disneyland.

What to See

Covering 56 hectares (138 acres), the Euro Disneyland theme park offers so much to see and do, particularly for a first-time visitor, that some careful planning is vital. As you make your way down Main Street, USA, and then wander off to explore the exciting worlds of Frontierland, Adventureland, Fantasyland and Discoveryland, it's all too easy to get completely lost if you don't have some prior idea of the lie of these lands.

It's best to accept right from the beginning that it is very unlikely you will be able to see everything on your first visit. Depending on how long you intend to stay at the theme park, you will want to pick out those attractions that are your first

---

Phone for Information
Although the information in this book is up-to-date at the time of going to press, details such as admission fees, prices, opening hours, public transport, shuttle and parking facilities, etc., will be subject to change. For the latest information contact Euro Disneyland **Guest Relations** at City Hall on Main Street, USA, tel. (33 1) 6474 3000.

---

choices. Save attractions you are less interested in until last, if there's time. Some will prefer to head straight for Pirates of the Caribbean, others to dream in Le Château de la Belle au Bois Dormant (Sleeping Beauty's Castle), others to step up the adrenaline with a ride on Big Thunder Mountain, saving tea with the Mad Hatter for the afternoon.

It is unlikely that you will be able to fit in more than seven or eight Euro Disneyland attractions on any one day and still have time for meals, a little shopping, and some relaxation too.

The most popular attractions often have long queues at certain times of day and you will probably prefer not to spend much time queuing up when you could be doing something else. This guidebook aims to help you make the right choices and get the most out of Euro Disneyland in the time available to you.

In Blueprint for a Perfect Trip (pp.105–25) you will find detailed practical information on transport, first-aid, lost property, baby-sitting facilities, etc., but to begin with here are some general hints on how to tackle Euro Disneyland.

When to Go?

Easter, July and August and other school-holiday periods are obviously the most popular times to visit the Euro Disney Resort. The crowds at these times may make it more difficult to see a maximum number of attractions without a great deal of queuing, but they also add to the festive atmosphere.

By the same token, the off-peak periods such as the winter months do have the disadvantages of earlier closing times and less frequent showings of night-time attractions such as the Main Street Electrical Parade and the fireworks displays.

Many people choose an off-peak period for a shorter first-time visit to get an overall sense of the place, then plan a longer second visit during the summer months.

One-Day Visits

Because of the sheer multitude of things to experience it is difficult to fit Euro Disneyland Park into a one-day visit. However, it can still be worthwhile if you follow the hints below on how to save time:

1. Get to the park before opening time so that you can make an early start and be at the front of the queues for the most popular attractions. Opening hours may vary from time to time, so check with the information desk at City Hall on Main Street, USA.

2. Have lunch early in order to avoid the midday crowds in the restaurants.

3. Plan to do your shopping while most other visitors are taking their meals – at lunch or dinner time, depending on how long you are staying. You can stow your purchases in coin-operated lockers under the Euro Disneyland Railroad's Main Street Station and pick them up on your way out.

How to Get There

If you are travelling by car you can reach the Euro Disney Resort via the A4 motorway east of Paris (Autoroute de l'Est) to the Parc Euro Disneyland exit. This leads right into the Euro Disneyland visitors' car park, with room for 11,500 cars. From there, you take the moving walkway to the theme park entrance located beneath the Disneyland Hotel. For disabled visitors using wheelchairs, a separate car park is available providing special access (other facilities for disabled visitors are detailed on p.115).

By train it's even simpler: via Paris's Gare de Lyon station, the eastbound RER rapid transit line takes you straight to the Euro Disney Resort entrance, at Marne-la-Vallée–Chessy station. From 1994 the high-speed TGV express will stop off at the theme park from the French provinces.

Children still love the classic Disney characters best of all.

Longer Visits

As far as the Euro Disneyland theme park itself is concerned, many of the tips for one-day visitors can usefully be applied to longer stays, too. But take advantage of your greater leisure time to enjoy the resort's other attractions outside the main park.

1. Go to most of your first-choice attractions very early, when they are least busy, so that

4. In summer you can visit some of the attractions after dinner and still have plenty of time to enjoy the spectacular Main Street Electrical Parade and the **32** fireworks.

you have time for a rather more relaxed tour of the park in the afternoon.

2. Because of the great popularity of the Main Street Electrical Parade in the evening, make sure that at least one member of your party can be there ahead of time to stake out a good kerbside viewing position.

3. However enthralling the attractions may be, intensive Euro Disneyland visits over a longer period can lead to bouts of sightseeing fatigue – plain 'visual overload'. People staying at Disney hotels can counter this by breaking up their visits with an afternoon change of pace at the golf course, tennis courts, swimming pool or health club, then continue refreshed for some evening fun back in the park.

4. The sightseeing can also be split up with an excursion or two to the attractions of the surrounding countryside. Guests staying at the Disney hotels can sign up for guided tours there, or drive their own or rented cars to Paris, the Champagne vineyards or the châteaux of Versailles, Fontainebleau and Vaux-le-Vicomte (see pp.96–104).

Entrance to Euro Disneyland Park

The car park walkway and the RER railway station both lead into Disney Square. Beyond a

---

A Few Dos and Don'ts

Clothing is naturally very casual at Euro Disneyland, but visitors must not go barefoot or bare-chested.

Some other pointers:

● Weather in the Paris region can be unpredictable, so unless there is a heatwave, do take along a sweater and some light rainwear.

● Despite the theme park's ingenious compact layout designed to minimize sore feet, some weariness is inevitable, so be sure to wear comfortable walking shoes. You may even want to pack a lighter spare pair for the evening if you are not going back to the hotel beforehand.

● Visitors may not bring their own food and drink into the theme park. A picnic area is available between the car park and the entrance to Euro Disneyland Park. Visitors can have their hand marked with a re-entry stamp when leaving for a picnic lunch so that they can get back in at no extra charge.

● Smoking is not allowed in queues or inside the attractions. Restaurants are divided into smoking and non-smoking sections.

pond and a flower portrait of your host, Mickey Mouse, is the entrance to Euro Disneyland, under Disneyland Hotel.

In the ticketing area, seven booths provide 42 windows for you to purchase your 'Passport' to the park. This gives access to all the attractions in Euro Disneyland Park without extra payment. (One exception: Frontierland's Rustler Roundup Shootin' Gallery, which costs 10 francs per game to discourage shooting enthusiasts from hogging their gun all day long!) When planning your budget, allow for food, drinks and shopping.

Exchange booths are available for converting foreign currency. Traveller's cheques and credit cards are also accepted.

Euro Disneyland Railroad

Through the turnstiles, the park begins at the 19th-century-style two-storey Main Street Station of the park's own railway – or 'Railroad' as this all-American steam train service is more appropriately named. Some visitors may like to start out with the 2.2 km (1.4 mile) trip around the park's periphery to get an overall first impression, saving the stroll up Main Street, USA for later.

The train stops in Frontierland and Fantasyland, with entertaining close-up views of park attractions on the way, before circling back to Main Street Station.

In line with Walt Disney's passion (see p.23) there are three trains, each meticulously reproducing designs of the 1880s, typical of the trains that chugged along branch-line railways and complete with cowcatchers, bells and whistles. They operate with real steam engines such as the Western-style green *W.F. Cody* (after Buffalo Bill), pulling carriages named *Durango*, *Wichita* and *Cheyenne*, or the blue presidential *G. Washington* at the head of carriages named *Boston*, *Philadelphia* and *Valley Forge*. Each carriage can hold 54 passengers. Notice the interiors' stylishly crafted fixtures, with bench-seats all facing into the park.

The train passes at a leisurely pace through the **Grand Canyon Diorama**. This is an attraction visible only from the train. One of the world's great natural wonders is presented with lifelike models of wild animals, bizarre rock formations, trees and foliage. As you pass through the different scenes, the Arizona daylight appears to change from dawn to sunset amid animal cries and bird calls.

One scene shows ancient Indian cliff dwellings abandoned to their present-day inhabitants – grey foxes, pack rats and coiled rattlesnakes. Other scenes show deer and raccoons foraging for food among the juniper trees while crows caw overhead, a den of cougar wildcats, and howling coyotes hunting wild turkeys as a storm breaks with thunder and forked lightning. Finally, after the storm, the sky is lit up by a double rainbow and glowing sunset while two pronghorn antelope rams prepare to do battle in the foreground.

Emerging from the Grand Canyon Diorama, you get a dramatic view across the Rivers of the Far West to Frontierland's major attraction, the **Big Thunder Mountain railroad** (see pp.46–8). Up in Adventureland, passengers catch a glimpse of the skeletons of three dastardly brigands and a couple of other scenes from the grand **Pirates of the Caribbean** attraction. In Fantasyland younger children's appetites are whetted by a close-up view of It's a **Small World** (see pp.68–70). The older crowd is likely to be tempted by the view of **Videopolis** in Discoveryland (see p.71).

Main Street, USA

The nostalgic world of Walt Disney's charmed imagination begins beyond Main Street Station. The sights and sounds of small-town America at the beginning of the 20th century are evoked by antiquated vehicles, old-fashioned shop fronts and the oom-pah-pah of a brass band, often with Mickey, Donald and the gang parading past quaint little shops along Main Street. All that and the fragrance of freshly baked chocolate-chip cookies, popcorn and sizzling hot dogs, too. At the far end there is a glimpse of the dreamy turrets, belfries and spires of Le Château de la Belle au Bois Dormant (Sleeping Beauty's Castle).

EURO DISNEYLAND

ADVENTURELAND

PIRATES
OF THE CARIBBEAN

ADVENTURE ISLE

LES VOY
DE PINO

LA CABANE DES
ROBINSON

BLANCHE-NE
ET LES SEPT NA

**FRONTIERLAND
DEPOT**

COTTONWOOD
CREEK RANCH

River Rogue Keelboats

BIG THUNDER
MOUNTAIN

Thunder Mesa

Libe
Cou

Riverboat
Landing

RIVERS OF THE FAR WEST

PHANTOM
MANOR

City
Hall

GRAND CANYON DIORAMA

FRONTIERLAND

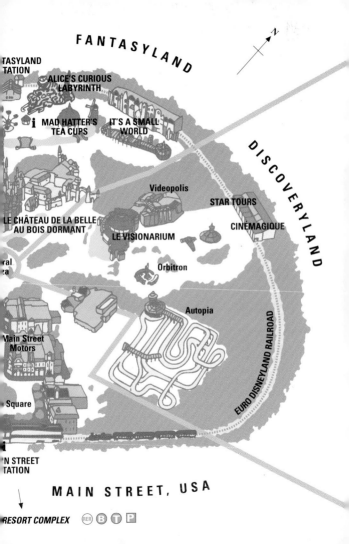

FANTASYLAND

TASYLAND
TATION

ALICE'S CURIOUS LABYRINTH

MAD HATTER'S TEA CUPS

IT'S A SMALL WORLD

DISCOVERYLAND

Videopolis

STAR TOURS

LE CHÂTEAU DE LA BELLE AU BOIS DORMANT

LE VISIONARIUM

CINÉMAGIQUE

ral
a

Orbitron

Autopia

Main Street Motors

EURO DISNEYLAND RAILROAD

Square

N STREET
TATION

MAIN STREET, USA

RESORT COMPLEX (RER) B T P

Town Square

As you come from the station **City Hall** is to the left, all-important for its information office. Multilingual staff here can tell you what's going on in all the 'lands', what times the shows start, what's open, and what's closed. You may enquire about lost children at City Hall, and if you have mislaid anything else, it's the site of the lost-property office (Lost and Found), too.

Across the square is home base for Main Street's collection of

A pensive moment for one of the Seven Dwarfs at Euro Disneyland.

vintage vehicles. Take a ride in an old police **paddy wagon**, a bright-red **fire engine**, an **omnibus**, a majestic **limousine** or one of three **horse-drawn streetcars** – choose among the *San Francisco*, *St Louis* or *Saratoga*. Each vehicle takes visitors on a trip to Central Plaza (or back from there).

Next to the Main Street Vehicles HQ is the **Ribbons & Bows Hat Shop**. At this Victorian-style lady's milliner's you can buy hats and hair accessories. Have your hat monogrammed in the rear of the shop, where old sewing machines whir away. Close by this shop is a rental service for children's pushchairs (strollers) and for wheelchairs, limited in number on a first-come, first served basis.

Next door to City Hall is **The Storybook Store**, designed like a small-town children's library and selling Disney books, records and video tapes. An animated Tigger (a favourite character from A.A. Milne's *Winnie the Pooh* and Disney's screen adaptation of the famous tale) is there to put a personalized stamp in any child's new book.

Up Main Street

On the left-hand side is the **Emporium**, a 19th-century department store. Period details include an overhead cable-driven money-

39

exchange system serving the cashier's office. The store sells specially designed Euro Disneyland clothing, jewellery, Paris souvenirs, Disney character toys and accessories.

Opposite the Emporium is **Town Square Photography**, displaying antique cameras, tintypes, daguerrotypes and a processing laboratory that demonstrates historical techniques. Inside you can buy film and a variety of other supplies, including Disney video films. You can also rent cameras (still and video), and have minor repairs done and photos developed. In one of the shop's alcoves, a **silhouette artist** will cut out your paper silhouette and frame it while you wait.

In the same block is the **Boardwalk Candy Palace**. Here you can see – and buy – saltwater taffy (a type of toffee) made in the shop's kitchen, just as it was 100 years ago in Atlantic City, New Jersey, a popular East Coast seaside resort.

Next door, **Disney Clothiers, Ltd** sells Mickey Mouse and Donald Duck outfits and other

A nostalgic recreation of smalltown America.

Disney clothing in a very gracious interior evoking the atmosphere of an elegant Victorian lady's apartment converted into a shop, with the daybed, fireplace, velvet curtains and player piano still there.

Main Street Motors

With its old petrol (or rather, gas) pump outside the showroom, you can't miss the chief attraction on the block. At Main Street Motors, gleaming vintage cars and motorbikes are on sale – along with various automobile memorabilia. Among the classics are a 1907 Reliable Dayton High Wheeler Model C and a 1911 Excelsior Auto-Cycle Model G, both guaranteed authentic. The vendor's gift of the gab demonstrates what a monumental role the used-car salesman has played in the success of the American economy.

Beyond the car showroom is **Harrington's Fine China & Porcelains**, selling just that and a selection of crystal, too, with Disney or non-Disney motifs. The atmosphere is most high class. In the rear of the shop you can watch as an expert hand-paints china. Located in the same store is **Disneyana Collectibles**, a treasure trove for the serious collector of Disney animation 'cels' (the celluloid drawing sheets used in the original animated films), rare books and limited-edition lithographs.

Harmony Barber Shop

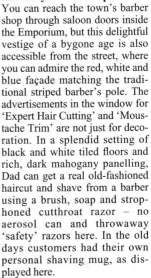

You can reach the town's barber shop through saloon doors inside the Emporium, but this delightful vestige of a bygone age is also accessible from the street, where you can admire the red, white and blue façade matching the traditional striped barber's pole. The advertisements in the window for 'Expert Hair Cutting' and 'Moustache Trim' are not just for decoration. In a splendid setting of black and white tiled floors and rich, dark mahogany panelling, Dad can get a real old-fashioned haircut and shave from a barber using a brush, soap and strop-honed cutthroat razor – no aerosol can and throwaway 'safety' razors here. In the old days customers had their own personal shaving mug, as displayed here.

As often as not, a lively barbershop quartet is on hand to keep the rest of the family entertained with a jolly selection of romantic melodies – it's not called Harmony Barber Shop for nothing! Shaving mugs, brushes and soap are on sale. Another feature is the hand-cranked telephone on the wall, a 1910-style party line on which you can listen in to the latest local news and gossip.

In the block beyond Liberty Court you will find a wide range of Disney toys, T-shirts and other gifts at **Disney & Co**, flanked by Walt's – an American Restaurant and Casey's Corner hot-dog shop (see p.90).

Central Plaza

The wheel-shaped plaza at the top of Main Street, USA serves as the hub of the park's five 'lands'. From here you can choose your next destination: clockwise from the left, **Frontierland**, **Advent-** ureland (see p.53), **Fantasyland** (see p.59) or **Discoveryland** (see p.70).

Frontierland

The frontier is of course that of the American West in the 19th century, when pioneers mined for gold or drove their cattle across the range. Frontierland offers you the chance to experience the thrills and dangers of those times with shooting practice at the

*Main Street, USA – all-American
tradition at the heart of Europe's
first Disney resort.*

**Rustler Roundup Shootin'
Gallery**, a bone-shaking ride on
Big Thunder Mountain railroad
or a fearsome visit to **Phantom
Manor**. There is also a more
easy-going time to be had with a
quiet steamboat cruise or canoe
trip on the **Rivers of the Far
West** before moseying on over
to the barbecue at **Cowboy
Cookout**.

The prevailing atmosphere of
Frontierland as you enter from
the Central Plaza hub is that of a
booming mining town after the
Forty-Niners struck it rich in California. (If you arrive by Euro
Disneyland Railroad at Frontierland Depot you can start out at
Cottonwood Creek Ranch.)

Thunder Mesa

Entrance from Central Plaza
to the town of Thunder Mesa   **43**

is via the timbered stockade of **Fort Comstock**. Across a wooden bridge over a pond, you see rough-hewn logpole gates flanked by a couple of three-storey blockhouses. On their upper landings are **telescopes,** through which you can get a first close-up of the mid-river islands beyond. In the centre of the stockade is a flagpole flying the United States banner of 1876, the 38-star Centennial Flag when Colorado joined the Union. At the water's edge a temporary-looking **Indian camp** has been set up with tepees, a campfire and a wooden travois sled.

As you enter town, **The Lucky Nugget Saloon** and other restaurants (see pp.90-92) are on your left and the shops of the **Thunder Mesa Mercantile Building** on your right. Here, near lifesize figures of Buffalo Bill and Kit Carson, you will find sturdy leather goods at **Tobias Norton & Sons – Frontier Traders**, and elegant Western clothing, from finely tooled boots to cowboy hats, at **Bonanza Outfitters** next door. Toys with a frontier motif are on sale at **Eureka Mining Supplies and Assay Office,** an

abandoned mining shack where miners used to buy their tools and bring their gold nuggets and dust to be weighed.

Rustler Roundup Shootin' Gallery

Right opposite the Thunder Mesa Building, a waterfront wharf

A jovial barber shop quartet and red and white striped pole are guarantees of a traditional haircut **44** *at the Harmony Barber Shop.*

housing 20 coin-operated shooting stands offers an irrestible chance for you to match your skills against the best guns in the West. The electronic shooting gallery, with its 74 cartoon-style targets, costs 10 francs – the only 'extra charge' among the park's attractions.

The trigger on your gun activates an infrared beam, which sets off a whole series of visual and sound effects. Targets spin, teeter, fall over, tremble, pop up or explode. Gunshots whistle, bang or go 'boing' on impact, a ricochet whines if you miss. The targets include cacti, dynamite

barrels, tin cans, vultures, prairie dogs, tombstones, weather vanes, lightning rods and a whisky still – particularly spectacular if you hit it.

 ## Big Thunder Mountain

A novel feature of this runaway mine train is that it plunges underwater before emerging to hurtle around the mountain island. On the way, you can explore the treacherous shafts and tunnels of a Wild West gold mine.

The train **loading area** is located just past the Rustler Roundup Shootin' Gallery, in the mainland office of the Big Thunder Mining Co – seven weather-beaten timbered buildings lit up in the evening by flickering miners' lanterns. Beside the foreman's headquarters and the Assay Office (for evaluating the ore) are the ore-milling equipment, water pump, air compressor, old ore wagons, steam tractor and water wheel. Not far from the furnace shed and hoist building (for raising ore from the mine) is the **outhouse**, with its traditional cut-out moon shape for the men's door and star for the women.

Here you board a mining train pulled by a decorative engine at the head of five wagons, each carrying six passengers held in by a lap-bar for safety. It starts off

downhill into a gloomy mine tunnel under the Rivers of the Far West, rising again past scores of bats' eyes glowing in the dark, phosphorescent whirlpools, stalactites and stalagmites. At the top of the rise a waterfall nearly (but never quite) drenches the passengers.

Now you're on the Big Thunder Mountain itself and the ride begins in earnest, plunging through tunnels and swerving

---

Wild West Peaks of Marne-la-Vallée

The silhouette of Big Thunder Mountain draws its inspiration directly from the dramatic mesa plateaux, sandstone pinnacles, canyons and natural arched bridges of Arizona and Utah. True to their Hollywood allegiances, Disney's landscapers 'borrowed' the Monument Valley landscape made famous by the Western films of director John Ford – *Stagecoach* and *She Wore a Yellow Ribbon*.

The 33 m (108 ft) high mountain is made from a concrete mix poured over a wire-meshed iron frame and covered with a ruddy-hued plaster to give it the distinctive rough sandstone texture of the American South West. Its slopes are dotted with characteristic cacti, sagebrush and pine.

From land agents to leather goods, Thunder Mesa Building offers something for everyone.

around corners at dizzying speeds. At **Foreboding Gorge**, the train picks up speed past cactus plants and twisted trees into a dense pine forest where a family of opossum is swinging from the branches. Then it splashes past **Mill Landing** where an ore wagon from a busted branch line dangles perilously over the raging waters of Mill Creek. At **Mill Camp** a goat is trying to tug a prospector's overalls from a clothes line, watched by laughing pack mules.

Mind your head in **Coyote Canyon**. Two howling coyotes, flashing danger lights and an overturned ore wagon warn passengers to duck as they pass into **Head-Knocker Tunnel**. Amid rumbles at the approach to **Big Thunder Mine**, the train begins to shake. Sticks of dynamite litter the track and a miner shouts: 'Fire in the hole!' Suddenly an explosion shakes the cave walls, timber shafts crash down and fire flashes light up veins of gold in the rock face while gold dust sprinkles down. Again the train narrowly escapes as the mine shaft collapses behind you.

Just when you think you're out of danger, the train plunges once more – into a cave full of **47** screeching bats. The wagons are about to sink into the flood, but everyone is pulled to safety, back at the Big Thunder Mining Co headquarters, for disembarkation.

Rivers of the Far West

For a more tranquil view of Big Thunder Mountain and the adjoining Wilderness Island, take a cruise on the waterway – either on a paddlewheel steamboat or keelboat, or in an Indian canoe that you paddle yourself. Nostalgic for his boyhood view of the Mississippi River when the family owned a Missouri farm, Walt Disney wanted a river theme in all his parks. This one borrows features from the Col-

orado, the Sacramento in California and the Rio Grande that winds through Colorado, New Mexico and Texas.

There are two **riverboats**: the *Mark Twain* sternwheeler, named after the great American humorist, and the *Molly Brown* sidewheeler, named after a heroic American pioneer who worked tirelessly to save fellow passengers on the sinking *Titanic* in 1912. They continue to operate after dark, with spotlights illuminating the shoreline. Board at the **Thunder Mesa Riverboat Landing** on the waterfront opposite the Last Chance Café (see p.91).

Two smaller **River Rogue Keelboats**, the rough, tough *Raccoon* and *Coyote,* (also operating after dark) have their landing-stage up at Smuggler's Cove beyond the Big Thunder mountain loading area. Out on the cove's promontory you can paddle, with two guides, in one of the 11 m (35 ft) **Indian Canoes**. They do not operate after dark, but have the advantage over the bigger vessels of being able to explore Big Thunder Mountain's caverns and negotiate the stone arches.

The steamboat cruise goes anticlockwise. The first landmark is **Smuggler's Cove**, sombre home of fur traders and river pirates. Notice in the dock for the keelboats that one of the older models has sprung a leak and sunk.

The landscape of **Wilderness Island** varies from arid sandstone

Big Thunder Mountain's rugged silhouette is a reminder of Hollywood's classic Westerns. **49**

to forest greenery, with waterfalls and groves of conifers and birch trees.

On the marshy mainland river bank is **Joe's Landing** where, near the cottonwood trees, a fisherman nods over his rod while his dog barks at the passing boats. **Settlers' Landing** provides a repair shop for the boats and grazing for a family of moose at the water's edge. Notice, too, the abandoned Conestoga wagon and two ox skeletons half-buried in the sand.

After rounding Wilderness Island, you pass the mainland's **Geyser Plateau** where steaming hot water spouts high in the air and natural mud pots bubble like those in Yellowstone National Park, Wyoming. Boot Hill cemetery lights up an eerie green at sunset – a good time to visit Phantom Manor next door.

Phantom Manor

Up on a hill overlooking the Rivers of the Far West, this grim mansion contains more ghosts than you would ever have thought possible. Home of one of Thunder Mesa's founding families during the gold rush, it fell into decay after the patriarch's daughter was jilted on her wedding day and never seen *alive* again. Go in through the manor gates, just past the Riverboat Landing, and with luck and many a spine-chilling adventure you may get out again.

The woes of the ill-fated Bride and the wickedness of her tormentor, the Phantom (with the voice of horror star Vincent Price) are displayed with the aid of 92 'Audio-Animatronic' characters, 54 animated props and countless special effects.

Visitors queue at the **Garden Pavilion**, already made nervous by the whispering wind, distant laughter and voices, and the clinking of glasses from a long-forgotten banquet. As you approach the house, peer at the

The Birth of
'Audio-Animatronics'

The special patented lifelike characters that are a unique feature of the Disney theme parks arose from Walt Disney's passion for mechanical toys. In the 1940s he experimented with mechanical puppets, inspired by the premise of his *Pinocchio* film. His 'Imagineer' experts filmed musical comedy dancer Buddy Ebsen to provide a versatile model for their puppets to imitate. They originally operated on a primitive combination of vacuum tubes and clockwork mechanisms.

Gradually, the 'Imagineers' developed an intricate system of pneumatic and hydraulic transmission, with hundreds of taped sound impulses activating everything from arm and mouth movements to the mere flicker of an eyelid. These could now be coordinated with pre-recorded dialogue, music and lighting.

'*Audio-Animatronics*', as the system became known, was first used for some exotic birds at the California Disneyland. The breakthrough came with the 1964 World's Fair in New York, where Disney created a lifesize President Abraham Lincoln talking, gesturing, changing facial expressions and moving his gaze around the audience. During try-outs, however, before the system was fully mastered, the 'President' occasionally went berserk, smashing his chair and endangering the engineers working on him. Finally the system was controlled and the '*Audio-Animatronics*' characters became 'almost like humans'. Euro Disneyland features many of the most sophisticated.

---

upper windows and you will see a dim light flickering and hear the faint sound of an old music box. Dark silhouettes of the Phantom and the wretched Bride are visible through the windows, green smoke puffs from the manor's chimneys, a dog howls, and a raven caws.

Once you are inside the **Foyer** the front doors creak shut behind you – no backing out now as the Phantom himself welcomes you and invites you through a concealed panel into the **Doorless Chamber**. Entrapped in this candlelit den, you realise there is no way out, no windows, no doors to be seen – just distorted portraits of the Bride, and a hanging corpse. But somehow, you do get out, and travel along a moving carpet to board one of the **Doom Buggies** that will take you through the house, at times swivelling around 180 degrees so that you are confronted with the next terrifying scene.

Escaping the shadowy clutches of a giant bat, you pass under a

from a chandelier above, two ghosts grimly toast the festivities. Reappearing in a bolt of lightning, the only one who seems to be having a good time – besides the audience – is the Phantom.

In the **Bride's Boudoir** there is a portrait of a beautiful young woman, but at the dressing table sits an old hag examining her reflection in the mirror, a fleshless skull.

Next you pass through french windows into a moonlit **Graveyard** where the Phantom leans on a shovel beside a freshly dug grave, a demon dog snarling nearby. Suddenly the Doom Buggies drop back into subterranean **catacombs** where skeletons are falling apart or trying to put themselves together again, one couple tugging at an arm bone in an ownership dispute.

balcony into a curtained archway where the Bride welcomes you. Follow her candelabra down a gloomy, cobwebbed, seemingly endless corridor. She disappears, but you go into the **Music Room** where a ghost plays the piano with a raven perched on the music holder. Doors begin to twist, there's a terrible hammering, the clock strikes 13, and grotesque eyes glow in the dark.

After a crystal-ball séance, you arrive at the **Wedding Reception** in the Grand Hall. Wedding guests waltz to music played by a cloaked organist with skulls flying from the organ pipes while,

The Buggies emerge in **Phantom Canyon**, a Western ghost town destroyed by an earthquake during a bank robbery, and you are caught in the crossfire between the ghosts of a lawman and a bandit. In an **Apothecary**, a nice-looking pharmacist takes a potion, turns into a horrible monster then, in a flash of light

52

and puff of smoke, returns to normal. The earthquake splits the **Saloon** in two, separating the piano player from the bartender and saloon girl, while a poker game continues – with invisible gamblers.

Back in the **Manor Garden** the skeletal Bride in her ragged wedding gown points to the exit through a mirror-lined passage. Rumbling and shaking just out of reach of the Phantom, the Buggies escape to the **Wine Cellar** ... for one last surprise.

After leaving Phantom Manor, visitors with a morbid sense of humour should walk around **Boot Hill cemetery** where the ornate crypt and crumbling gravestones have some surprising epitaphs, such as:

A NEAR-SIGHTED MINER
IN SHAFT 39
LIT HIS CIGAR
AND BLEW UP THE MINE.

Cottonwood Creek Ranch

Up near the Frontierland Depot railway station is a model working ranch, with feeding sheds, stables, corrals and, nearby, a restaurant, the **Cowboy Cookout Barbecue** (see p.91). They stand amid groves of cottonwood and chaparral. In the shingle-roofed shack of the **Woodcarver's Workshop** you can watch a craftsman carving barnyard animals. His live models are over in **Critter Corral** where children can stroke the rabbits in their hutch, see 20 goats in a shelter and visit the chicken coop and pen.

Take a look at the **Frontierland Depot**. In this typical country railway station you can peer into the stationmaster's office with its telegraph key, desk and pot-bellied stove. Notice, too, the freight house and redwood watertower with its spout leaning out over the track.

Across from the barbecue, near Smuggler's Cove, the **Pueblo Trading Post** demonstrates the crafts and sells the wares of Navajo and Hopi Indians. In a structure of rough stone and adobe, you can buy turquoise and silver jewellery, hand-woven baskets, pottery, hand-loomed rugs, beaded clothes and kachina ancestral-spirit dolls. Indian artisans are on hand to demonstrate rug-making and basket-weaving.

Adventureland

This land takes you to the world of buccaneers, castaways and travellers to faraway places. As well as exploring the island home of the Swiss Family Robinson and joining in bloodthirsty fights among the Pirates of the

Caribbean, you can enjoy the colour, fragrance and spices of shops and restaurants (see p.92).

Adventureland Bazar

The gateway to Adventureland from Central Plaza looks like a fortified desert city in the Middle East or India's Rajasthan. Go through the decorative arch with its sandstone towers on each side, and seven onion domes beyond is an Oriental bazaar straight out of the *Arabian Nights*.

The courtyard is surrounded by five shops, each displaying its wares – carpets, brassware or other ornaments – beneath brightly coloured awnings. They are known here by their French names, as in North Africa.

L'Echoppe d'Aladin (Aladdin's Shop) sells jewellery. Over the entrance, a tiger and some monkeys fly out of an upstairs window on a magic carpet. **La Reine des Serpents** (The Serpent Queen) takes its name from a character in the *Arabian Nights* – a sculpture of this beautiful woman with a serpent's body is suspended from the shop's ceiling. Toys, statuettes and small trinkets are on sale here. **Le Chant des Tam-Tams** (Song of the Tam-Tams) sells East African carved masks, wooden animals, basketware and clothes. At **La Girafe Curieuse** (The Curious Giraffe) you will find safari wear

– shirts, shorts, pith helmets and jungle boots. A tree is growing through the middle of the shop where a giraffe's head is nibbling at the leaves. There are gifts from Morocco, Egypt and India on sale at **Les Trésors de Schéhérazade** (The Treasures of Sheherazade) – lanterns, brass bells, dolls, clothing, etc. The shop has scimitars stuck in the ceiling, left behind by the enemies of Sinbad the Sailor.

Over to the left facing Adventure Isle, on the border with Frontierland, is **Trader Sam's Jungle Boutique**. It has an African-style bamboo-framed thatched roof on wooden posts and walls of raffiatied bamboo in bold geometric patterns.

Adventure Isle

The island is connected to the mainland by several bridges. One sways above a waterfall, another bounces and bobs across barrels – but for those who cannot take too much adventure in their Adventureland there is also a conventional bridge. Full of creeks and lagoons, caves and hills, with swaying palms, banana plants and bamboo, Adventure Isle is shared by several grand tales, all of which have inspired popular Disney films. On the south side (signposted in French), there is La Cabane des Robinson, the tree house described by Johann David Wyss in *Swiss Family Robinson*

Adventureland – from exotic desert city to the challenges of Adventure Isle.

in 1813, while the north side (signposted in English) is devoted to the exploits of Robert Louis Stevenson's *Treasure Island* (1883) and the pirates of J.M. Barrie's *Peter Pan*, spilling over from Fantasyland.

La Cabane des Robinson

La Cabane des Robinson (Swiss Family Robinson's Tree House) is built in a splendid replica of a giant spreading banyan tree. The family made this their home after

being shipwrecked in the South Seas while fleeing the hardships of the Napoleonic Wars. They used débris from the ship to build the tree house.

Its four levels are reached by makeshift stairs spiralling into the upper branches. At ground level are the **library and kitchen**. On the second level is the **family room**, where a hand-pumped organ salvaged from the ship plays a jolly Swiss polka. The **parents'** and **sons' rooms** are up on the third and fourth levels. Higher still, telescopes look out to **Pegleg Point** and, of interest to parents, the **Explorers Club** restaurant (see p.92).

The rooms are each adorned by the father's pious descriptions. For example: 'Our Kitchen and dining room, complete with running water, volcanic stone hearth and oven-utensils of our own making. Salvage from wrecked ship, plus nature's bounty and my

An artist's impression of Adventureland, with the tree house in the foreground.

good wife's cooking, amply fulfil our wants.' Running water is provided by a rope pulley and an ingenious water wheel with bamboo cups carrying the water from the stream up to bamboo pipes which pour into the sinks.

Be sure to visit **Le Ventre de la Terre** (The Root Cellar), the cave where the family stores its food and belongings in bamboo cages.

Ben Gunn's Cave

Take the floating barrel bridge or suspension bridge to the north side of the island where young Jim Hawkins and old Long John Silver vied for the cave's hidden treasure. The underground hunt is conducted amid the sounds of bats and rats and ghostly pirates singing old sea shanties. Five different paths approach the cave, one leading to a bottomless pit, another across a rickety bridge. Spiral down to the **Dead Man's Maze** of stalactites and stalagmites and to the skeletons and glowing bats' eyes in the **Keelhaul Caverns**. Ben Gunn's treasure chest of precious gems, bejewelled sabres and rapiers, and other spoils of battle make it all worth while.

Skull Rock and Captain Hook's Pirate Ship

Rising 12 m (39 ft) above **Cannonball Cove** is a great monolith shaped like a giant skull. Children can climb up inside the rock and look through the 'mouth' where water runs between the teeth. Higher up, through the eye sockets, is a fine view over Captain Hook's Pirate Ship.

Anchored in Cannonball Cove, the 25 m (82 ft) long ship has a counter-service café below decks, offering crocodile sandwiches (that's the shape, not the filling), macaroons, snacks and soft drinks. On the upper decks, reached by an elevated gangplank, children can play among the rigging and iron canons or take the ship's wheel.

Pirates of the Caribbean

At the far end of Adventureland is one of the most popular of all Disney theme park attractions, housed in a massive greystone fortress under pirate attack. Over 100 characters and animals are featured, most of them '*Audio-Animatronics*' figures. The queuing area in a rocky grotto provides a none too reassuring first view of the pirate crew's quarters, a makeshift pub with skeletons and the remains of shipwrecks. Visitors start off with a nocturnal boat trip to the white sand beach of a Caribbean island bathed in moonlight, to the sound of crickets chirping and tropical birdsong. Mum and Dad may want to make a mental note to book a table at the nearby **Blue Lagoon Restaurant** (see p.92).

The boats are then hoisted from the cargo deck to the fort's upper level and back in time to the pirates' historic battles. Watch their bombardment of the **flooded fort**, with a ship's cat clinging to wreckage in a whirlpool and swashbuckling pirates swinging from the ship's mast. Others, in prison, are trying to lure the keys away from a guard dog. Suddenly your boat plunges through a hole blasted in the fort wall and into the midst of a new battle with cannonballs flying thick and thin.

In a **Caribbean town** the mayor is being dunked in a well to force him to reveal where the treasure is. At an **Auction** the pirates are bidding for the prettiest girls. Amid more swordfights, looting and carousing, one pirate chases a girl around town while an old woman beats off another with her broom. Musicians launch into a rollicking version of 'Yo Ho – A Pirate's Life for Me'.

The city duly catches fire, the arsenal explodes and you are blown back through a time-tunnel into the present, to **Hurricane Lagoon**. Here, a rainstorm leaves the wreck manned by yet another pirate-skeleton. In the **Treasure Chamber** a skeleton has been left to contemplate the jewels and coins he cannot enjoy. There's more booty in the **Captain's Quarters**, where you are lulled by the serenade of a ghostly harpsichord. Back in the **Crew's Quarters** long-dead buccaneers are downing a last rum, and a talking skull shows you the way out.

Outside the fort, **Le Coffre du Capitaine** (The Captain's Chest)

This deserted fort is the scene of a swashbuckling attack by the Pirates of the Caribbean.

is a shop, perhaps converted from an old inn, where you can buy pirate figures, model ships, muskets and cutlasses.

Fantasyland

The fairy-tale attractions here appeal more to younger children, and are mostly inspired by the classic Disney animated features. Dominated by Le Château de la Belle au Bois Dormant (Sleeping Beauty's Castle), the land is knee-deep in golden pixie dust. Visit Snow White and the Seven Dwarfs, follow Pinocchio to Pleasure Island and back, fly with Peter Pan or Dumbo, explore Alice's maze in Wonderland and then sing along with the children of It's a Small World.

Le Château de la Belle au Bois Dormant

In homage to Frenchman Charles Perrault, who made the tale *Sleeping Beauty* world famous, the castle is known at Euro Disneyland as Le Château de la Belle au Bois Dormant. The special importance that Walt Disney attached to such fairy tales is reflected in the pride of place given to the castle, centrepiece not only of Fantasyland but of the whole theme park. It is the first Disney building you see from the main road to the park, and it draws you

like a magnet as soon as you set foot on Main Street, USA.

The castle's stone tracery, balconies and flying buttresses, 16 towers, turrets and spires, the weather vanes and pennants (notice the D for Disney) are a triumphant combination of feudal castle, Gothic monastery and Renaissance palace. The dreamlike architecture is based on Eyvind Earle's design for the Disney animated classic, *Sleeping Beauty*. Its noble artistic pedigree draws, said Earle, on images from Jan Van Eyck, Pieter Bruegel, Albrecht Dürer, Botticelli, and the

---

Optical Magic

Two little details in Le Château de la Belle au Bois Dormant show how Disney's theme parks are conceived like a film set. The whole edifice has been 'heightened', making the tallest tower – 45 m (147 ft) – seem much taller, by the cinematic technique known as forced perspective. The walls are made of stones cut in sizes graduated from large at the foundations to smaller at the top of battlements and balconies.

Using another ingenious special effect, the central oval stained glass over the Gothic archway is in fact a 'polage' window, which changes scenes constantly.

famous 14th-century illuminated manuscripts of *Les Très Riches Heures du Duc de Berry*. The spiralling pyramidal effect also owes something to the silhouette of France's Mont St Michel.

As you approach across Central Plaza, notice the loving details enhancing the fairy-tale atmosphere. In front of the castle, topiary artists have sculpted Arizona cypresses and yew trees into cubes. On a grassy knoll west of the castle a waterfall pours into the moat. To the east, via a wooden footbridge, is the Wishing Well from *Snow White and the Seven Dwarfs*.

Inside the castle the vaulted ceiling is bright with coloured banners. A spiral staircase leads to an upper gallery with stone sculptures and bas-reliefs from *Sleeping Beauty* – squirrels, birds and fairies. Up in the **Castle Gallery**, scenes from the film are depicted in tapestries made by artisans from the celebrated region of Aubusson and nine stained-glass windows – real leaded glass fashioned by experts from London cathedrals, not cellophane from Hollywood. Here a melody wafts through the air –

Le Château de la Belle au Bois Dormant – spellbinding symbol of the Disney magic.

Tchaikovsky's *Sleeping Beauty* ballet.

On the east side of the castle **La Boutique du Château** specializes in holiday gifts – for Easter, Christmas, etc. – arrayed on trees beneath a barrel-vaulted ceiling. An ornate stone fireplace shows Sleeping Beauty's forest friends, a chipmunk, rabbits, an owl and other birds.

Nearby, **Le Théâtre du Château** (the Castle Theatre) stages open-air shows in a miniature version of the gardens of Versailles. There are sets resembling pop-up books, which are used to relate the story of Sleeping Beauty.

Down on the ground floor on the left of the great hall, **Merlin l'Enchanteur** (Merlin's Shop) is housed in the sorcerer's studio, complete with astrolabes, flying machine, beakers, flasks, test tubes, and skeletons from his less successful experiments. On sale are gifts of a more or less scientific bent, natural or supernatural – kaleidoscopes, prisms, crystal and glassware, sculptures, pewter and jewellery.

From Merlin l'Enchanteur, take the stairs down to **La Tanière du Dragon** (The Dragon's Lair) – a dungeon where the snoring, grumbling monster lies in a shallow, foggy pool, occasionally awaking to growl, hiss and snort smoke **61** through his nostrils, as any self-respecting dragon should.

A popular show for children is **Excalibur**, the Sword in the Stone ceremony held in the castle's main courtyard where King Arthur's sword rests on an anvil attached to a rock. A fanfare played by nine liveried trumpeters and nine drummers heralds the arrival of the great wizard Merlin. He does a few tricks and then announces his quest for a king or queen for the day to replace Arthur, who is taking a 24-hour sabbatical. A couple of strong men are unable to move the sword, but an unbelievably virtuous little boy or girl does manage it, is given a golden crown and a commemorative parchment scroll, and sets off a couple of doves to proclaim the good news.

Fantasyland Shops
In this fairyland a block of village shops and restaurants stretches out from the right of Sleeping Beauty's Castle. The hostesses of

Its fairy-tale buildings and enchanting merry-go-round endear Fantasyland to younger children.

La Confiserie des Trois Fées (Three Fairies' Sweetshop) are Sleeping Beauty's three fairy godmothers, Fauna, Flora and Merryweather. Here, lollipops grow from trees and every basket, barrel, nook and cranny is spilling over with chocolate gold coins, gingerbread men, nougat, nuts and Disney candy.

Tendrils from a giant green beanstalk grow out of the façade of **Sir Mickey's**, a clothes, souvenir and toy shop. **La Ménagerie du Royaume** (Royal Menagerie) sells high-class Disney dolls and merry-go-round figurines. At **La Chaumière des Sept Nains** (Seven Dwarfs' Cottage), you'll find stuffed toys and, across a little bridge leading to the Evil Queen's Castle, Disney-character clothing. Among its clothing, **Le Brave Petit Tailleur** (The Brave Little Tailor) makes a speciality of Disney-character hats. Behind the shops are two restaurants, **Auberge de Cendrillon** (Cinderella Inn) and **Pizzeria Bella Notte** (see pp.92–3).

Le Carrousel de Lancelot

Dominating the square outside the shops is this classic merry-go-round boasting 86 painted horses

and a couple of chariots seating six.

Blanche-Neige et Les Sept Nains

As you leave Le Château de la Belle au Bois Dormant you will see on the left the forbidding grey brick abode of the Evil Queen, who is peering from an upper balcony. The attraction based on *Snow White and the Seven Dwarfs* (*Blanche-Neige et les Sept Nains*) the well-known German fairytale told by the Brothers Grimm, starts out in the **Evil Queen's Dungeon**. She is working up her abominable potions and preparing the shiny red apple, one bite of which and, as it says in her magic book, 'the victim's eyes will close forever in the sleeping death'.

In a forest clearing outside the **Dwarfs' Cottage**, visitors board one of the Dwarfs' mine cars for a guided tour. The first view of the cottage shows it in a terrible mess, but being cleaned up by squirrels and birds under the supervision of Snow White. In the Dwarfs' band, Grumpy is on organ, Happy on bass, Sleepy on violin, Doc on mandolin and Bashful on concertina. Dopey, on Sneezy's shoulders, is gallantly offering to dance with Snow White. A happy scene, if the Evil Queen with her pet raven were **64** not peeping in.

To the music of 'Heigh Ho, Heigh Ho, it's off to work we go', next stop is the **Diamond Mine** with its gems glittering along the walls and piled high in the barrels. A runaway mine car narrowly misses you and careers on into the **Queen's Castle**, where the queen is doing her 'Mirror, mirror, on the wall' routine, changing from an ice-cold beauty to a hideous crone. You can see a few skeletons of her past victims and a cauldron is bubbling away to poison the apples. The queen offers you one – want a bite? The apple turns into a skull.

In the **Haunted Forest** you pass nasty gnarled trees, crocodile logs and bats flitting around. The queen-cum-witch comes out of the Dwarfs' cottage with her apple, and the seven dwarfs follow her up a cliff. She tries to crush them with a boulder but a flash of lightning puts an end to her evil. There is a happy ending, of course, as Snow White and her Prince Charming go off to their castle with the Dwarfs waving goodbye.

Les Voyages de Pinocchio

Next door to the Snow White attraction, you can follow this Italian fairy tale (by Carlo Collodi) comfortably seated in hand-crafted woodcarver's carts. The adventure begins in **Pinocchio's**

Village, which has typical Italian cottages and shops, and the woodcarver Geppetto's workshop. The wicked Stromboli's puppet wagon is parked nearby. In **Stromboli's Theatre** Pinocchio is singing and dancing with other puppets. In the theatre's prison-like **Backstage** area, our hero, with a longer nose, is locked in a birdcage. Notice one of the puppets has been chopped up and thrown away.

On the road to **Pleasure Island** you are lured into the fair by Foulfellow the Fox and Gideon the Cat to see a Ferris wheel and merry-go-round made of candy-cane, a roller coaster and hot-air balloon, and a strength-tester with a donkey's head in place of the bell. Amid the diabolical laughter of shifty gamblers in the **Eight-Ball Pool Hall** is a menacing giant Jack-in-the-Box. Watch as Pinocchio's pal Lampwick grows the ears and tail of a donkey. The evil Coachman makes a grab at you to join the other donkey-boys being sent off to the Salt Mines.

Make your escape with Pinocchio and Jiminy Cricket and sail home, after an attack by Monstro the Whale. Back in **Geppetto's House** the Blue Fairy turns Pinocchio into a real boy and, in the **Toy Shop Finale**, the other toys also come to life and the pendulums and clocks go cuckoo.

La Bottega di Geppetto, a toy shop modelled on Geppetto's workshop, sells cuckoo clocks, music boxes, mechanical toys and fantasy chess sets. Next door is a fast-food restaurant, **Au Chalet de la Marionnette** (see p.93).

Peter Pan's Flight

A covered wooden bridge takes you from Pinocchio's village to the opening setting for British writer J.M. Barrie's marvellous story of the Darling family: a quaint English home with a brown shingled roof, brick chimneys and half-timbered stone walls. Enter through a clocktower to a typical English port.

There, you board miniature pirate galleons to fly off over the rooftops and smoking chimneys of London to the **Darling children's nursery**. Wendy is telling her brothers, John and Michael, about Peter Pan, the flying boy who never grows up, and his pixie friend, Tinker Bell, when suddenly Peter himself flies through the room and out of the window. Everyone follows him around Big Ben, along the Thames to Tower Bridge and up to 'The Second Star on the Right'.

Once over **Never Land** you can see Mermaid Lagoon, an Indian camp and Captain Hook's red and gold galleon in Cannibal

Cove. He fires a cannon in greeting. Down at **Skull Rock** Wendy is being forced to walk the plank with John and Michael tied to a mast. Peter Pan duels with Captain Hook while the Crocodile waits patiently below for the loser. With wand and pixie dust, Tinker Bell turns the galleon to gold and you splash through a waterfall down into **Mermaid Lagoon**, all safe and happy. Time for a snack next door at **Toad Hall Restaurant** (see p.93).

Dumbo the Flying Elephant

Across from Peter Pan's Flight, a circus wagon provides the entrance to this delightful aerial merry-go-round on which elephants really do fly. The festivities are conducted by Dumbo's pal, Timothy Mouse, rotating atop a hot-air balloon. The whole thing is designed like a giant wind-up toy, with brass gears, spinning pinwheels and a big turning-key. Riders can vary their height above the ground with a lever inside each Dumbo elephant.

Take a ride on Dumbo the Flying Elephant, supervised by Timothy Mouse, or go for a spin in the Mad Hatter's Teacups.

Alice's Wonderland

Based on Walt Disney's 1951 film adaptation of Lewis Carroll's classic studies of the absurd, *Alice in Wonderland* and *Through the Looking-Glass*, **Mad Hatter's Tea Cups** offers you an appropriately dizzying ride as you sit in one of 18 giant tea cups. The tea cup turns one way while its 'saucer' spins in the other direction. Even though you can control the spinning speed with a disk inside the cup, it's enough to drive you as mad as a hatter.

Alice's Curious Labyrinth is altogether a more leisurely experience. With their sights set firmly on a big grinning Cheshire Cat and later the Queen of Hearts Castle, visitors walk through the Wonderland maze in small groups around yew hedges and topiaries. It all begins in a tunnel as the White Rabbit patters past overhead, muttering, 'Oh, dear, I'm late, I'm late, for a very important date.'

You pass signs saying 'This Way', 'That Way', 'Go Back' – none of them very helpful, least of all the Cheshire Cat suggesting, 'You can go this way or that way.' When you come across the Caterpillar sitting on top of a **Giant Mushroom** you suddenly feel as if you have shrunk. There 67 is the famous **Caucus Race** with a splashing musical fountain before you reach the first destination, a great **Cheshire Cat** with hedgework stripes and the famous grin set in gravel. This first part is easy, and after completing it you can go off for a snack at **March Hare Refreshments** (see p.93).

The second part is more challenging, setting up more dead ends, but it is well worth the effort. The Queen of Hearts bellowing 'Off with their heads!' and her Playing Card soldiers running aimlessly about are more hindrance than help. Finally you round a bend and, through a guard of honour formed by crazy Playing Cards, you reach the **Queen of Hearts Castle**. It's a surreal purple cobblestone affair wherein all is illusion. Here, with the aid of distorting mirrors on the ground floor, and down below in the **Ames Room**, there is a riot of forced perspective and exaggerated proportions, causing children to grow into giants and adults to shrink to midgets.

It's a Small World

From Alice's Curious Labyrinth, walk past **The Old Mill** restaurant (see p.93) to a great fountain and the multi-coloured towers of It's a Small World – the Euro Disneyland musical tribute to the children of the world. Canal boats cruise past models of Paris's Eiffel Tower, London's Big Ben and Tower Bridge, Pisa's Leaning Tower, onion domes of the Middle East, skyscrapers of the USA and the pagodas of China.

Turrets of the bizarre Queen of Hearts Castle.

The centrepiece of the attraction is a **Clocktower**, which marks every quarter of an hour with a bustling parade of lively animated figures – flags wave, balls bounce, the sun rotates, an hour-glass turns upside down, propellers spin and a soldier blows his trumpet while other musicians from all over the world play. In a show using hundreds of '*Audio-Animatronics*' characters, toys and other models, you cruise past the children of every continent singing in nine different languages:

'It's time we're aware

It's a small world after all.'

There are children from all over the world – Norwegian skaters, Greek shepherds, Russian Cossacks and Balinese fandancers, Chinese children flying kites, Yemeni and Saudi girls singing in Arabic, an Israeli girl singing in Hebrew, Australian boomerang-throwers, an Argentinian gaucho, a Chilean flautist, Hopi Indians, and even an American football player. The grand finale unites them all.

Nearby, **The World Chorus** continues the theme with ingenious use of the latest electronics and synthetic imagery developed by the French communications industry. Again with children at the centre of the attraction – a boy in white tie and tails is conducting the Chorus from inside the Eiffel Tower – the most advanced technology is given a **69** warm, human, even humorous dimension.

Discoveryland

The architecture is all nuts and bolts. In place of the frills, flounces and furbelows of the other lands, Discoveryland has flashing lights and laser beams, at their most spectacular at night time. This land takes a sharp look at the technology of our ancestors, our contemporaries and our grandchildren. At Le Visionarium it examines the way in which the inspired dreamers of the past envisaged the future. Star Tours offers Disney's and George Lucas's humorous vision of space exploration in the future. Two of today's audio-visual wizards, singer Michael Jackson and film director Francis Ford Coppola, join forces at CinéMagique. Videopolis provides an avant-garde arena for mind-bending live music and video shows.

Le Visionarium

This is a cinema with a difference. With a film made by a nine-camera set-up known as '9-Eye', a process known as *Circle-Vision 360* projects its images on nine interlocking screens completely surrounding the audience. You stand at a railing in the centre of the auditorium to watch a 20-minute feature, *From Time to Time,* which combines 'Audio-Animatronics' characters with live actors, computerized special effects, and interaction from the audience. You need that rail to hold on to for some of the more exciting effects.

The story shows the great French adventure writer Jules Verne, played by Michel Piccoli, taking a time machine into the past (an idea borrowed from fellow visionary H.G. Wells) to the age of the dinosaurs, then travelling all the way back again to the present and on to the distant future. Throughout the journey the audience is confronted with the stunning inventions of the human race. The action switches from Paris to London to Vienna to Moscow and the Bahamas, and features Leonardo da Vinci, played by Franco Nero; a talented seven-year-old boy named Mozart; and, at Paris's Charles de Gaulle Airport, a baggage-handler played by Gérard Depardieu.

The adjoining **Constellations** shop sells Disney-character toys with a futuristic touch.

Orbitron

Pilot your own spaceship here, amid the twinkling lights of the galaxy outside Videopolis. Choose one of 12 rockets that whirl around and through a cosmos of planets and other astral bodies, in an attraction inspired by Leonardo da Vinci.

Autopia

Here, on the far east side of the Orbitron, is your chance to drive a prototype racing car of the 21st century around a dream landscape reaching even further into the future. There are more hairpin bends and loops than the Grand Prix tracks at Monaco, Nuremburgring and Silverstone combined. (The cars do not reach their full speed potential.)

Videopolis

A gigantic airship, the Hypérion, invites you into the great green-girdered hangar that is in fact an enclosed amphitheatre for live stage shows, night-time dancing and rock and pop music concerts. Audiences are lured in by criss-crossing beacon lights and chase lights flashing along the ground to the entrance. Drawing again on the passions of science-fiction writer Jules Verne, the place is alive with landmark inventions of the past – the first aircraft, hot-air balloons, antique bicycles. **Café Hypérion** provides hamburgers for the hurried.

The gleaming pinnacle of the Orbitron, which whirls you around the cosmos.

Star Tours

For many, this attraction, located on the far side of the Euro Disneyland Railroad, is likely to be the most exciting in Discoveryland. The astonishingly realistic impact of being propelled through space is engineered by professional flight-simulator equipment. The seat belt you put on is not there just for fun – there's no danger, but you really do feel you need to be strapped in once you're aboard a 'Star-speeder'.

Race into the 21st century in style at Autopia.

Not that it isn't a lot of fun anyway. George Lucas's *Star Wars* characters, R2D2 and C3P0, are there to provide the laughs. Passing into an ultra-modern functional-looking 'factory', you meet the fat and thin robots in the **Maintenance Hangar** where they are now organizing intergalactic flights for their new 'spaceline' company. Take a look, too, at the 'robot droids' being put together in the **Droidnostics Centre**.

On board the **Starspeeder** you meet a new robot, Captain RX24, or Rex, as he likes to be known. Trouble is, this is the captain's maiden flight, and everything goes wrong. In front of you is a 'windshield' that is in fact a 70-mm film of the space through which you are travelling. Add to that the hyper-realistic flight simulation reproducing effects of G-force (gravity) acceleration, sudden deceleration, and propulsion to one side or the other, and you're suddenly glad you have that seat belt. Rex is a nice guy, but he's not a very skilled pilot.

Videopolis is the venue for spectacular live shows.

CinéMagique

This cinema is reached by a canopied entrance under the Railroad. You are given 3-D glasses as you go in. Francis Ford Coppola has used the latest audio-visual techniques to direct Michael Jackson as 'Captain EO.'

This musical science-fiction feature stars Jackson as a spaceship captain – just think what *Star Trek*'s Captain Kirk would have been like if he could sing and dance. Together with Fuzzball, Hooter and Geex, he is on his way to save a miserable planet from the clutches of its extremely nasty Supreme Leader, played by Angelica Huston. All it takes is a little latterday rock 'n' roll. Jackson sings 'We Are Here to Change the World' and 'Another Part of Me'.

On the other side of the tracks the **Star Traders** shop, attached to a future Railroad station, is open for business, with very hi-tech *Star Wars* décor of solar panels and grey metal. It sells futuristic toys, games and souvenirs.

73

What to Do

The great thing about the Euro Disney Resort is that there is much to see besides all the theme park attractions and plenty to do besides going on your favourite rides. Take time off to enjoy not only some shopping but also the sports opportunities and day- and night-time shows laid on by the Festival Disney entertainment complex and the Disney hotels outside the park.

Shopping

Because of the way the Disney designers have integrated many of the shops with the park's attractions, the chapter on What to See already provides detailed descriptions of those situated inside the park. Below is a reminder of the range of goods available in the park, in addition to the many other shops you can find attached to the resort's hotels and Festival Disney.

Toys

At first glance, Euro Disneyland itself looks like one giant toy shop. The choices are endless.

An affectionate peck on the nose for Goofy.

but Fantasyland is perhaps the best place to start: **Sir Mickey's**, **La Ménagerie du Royaume** (Royal Menagerie) and **La Chaumière des Sept Nains** (Seven Dwarfs' Cottage) all sell stuffed Disney toys. **La Boutique du Château**, right beside Le Château de la Belle au Bois Dormant (Sleeping Beauty's Castle), specializes in gifts for seasonal holidays. Mechanical toys and cuckoo clocks are the main feature at **La Bottega di Geppetto**. Things get more futuristic,

While browsing on Main Street pause to admire the quaintly old-fashioned shop fronts.

positively hi-tech, at Discoveryland's **Star Traders**, but one of the biggest toy displays in the park is **Constellations**, leading to Videopolis.

There are more toy shops at Festival Disney and at each of the six Disney hotels and Camp Davy Crockett.

Clothing
A major attraction for fashion-conscious shoppers at Euro Disneyland is the large range of Western-style clothing. You'll find cowboy boots, Stetson hats, shirts, jeans, finely tooled belts and other leatherwear in Frontierland's **Thunder Mesa Mercantile** building.

At Festival Disney the **Buffalo Trading Company** also sells first-class leather goods, clothes and other memorabilia of the Wild West. Athletics and sports clothing and equipment are on sale at **Team Mickey**, adorned with Disney character logos. The **Surf Shop** offers swim- and beachwear and other casual clothing, while the **Streets of America Shop** stocks high-fashion designer clothes in a décor highlighted by the great landmarks of New York, New Orleans and San Francisco.

You'll find safari clothing at Adventureland's **La Girafe Curieuse** (The Curious Giraffe).

Americana

Many of the shops celebrate the more genteel, old-fashioned American way of life with goods like the shaving mugs and soaps you can buy at the **Harmony Barber Shop**, fancy hats (monogrammed free of charge) at the **Ribbons & Bows Hat Shop**, saltwater taffy at the **Boardwalk Candy Palace** – all on Main Street, USA. The sweets at Fantasyland's **La Confiserie des Trois Fées** are pretty good, too.

Movie Memorabilia

In a shop designed like a film set, Festival Disney's **Hollywood Pictures** specializes in books, photographs, posters and other paraphernalia from the history of the cinema, plus many souvenirs from the Disney studio. The pride of **Disneyana Collectibles**, on Main Street, USA, must be the original celluloid drawings used in the Disney animated features.

Crafts

At Frontierland's **Woodcarver's Workshop** you can buy hand-carved animals that are made while you watch. Also in Frontierland, the **Pueblo Trading Post** sells Mexican jewellery and Indian baskets and rugs – some of them, too, made right there in the shop.

Photographic Products

For film, cameras (video and still) and other photographic equipment, go to Town Square Photography on Main Street, USA. It does minor repairs, too, and hires out cameras for 50F per day and video cameras for 300F per day.

Sports

The facilities for practising your favourite sports just inside the Euro Disney Resort are first class. They range from the mind-boggling electronic games in the hotels to the highly professional golf course (with a light Disney touch) south of the main resort complex.

Golf

The 18-hole golf course, with another nine holes set to open in 1993, is known French-style as **Golf Euro Disney**. Signposted all the way, it is located just outside the resort's Boulevard Circulaire between the hamlets of Magny-le-Hongre and Bailly-Romainvilliers. Golf carts are used on the course. Golfing equipment is on sale at **Goofy's Pro Shop**, and the Club House serves snacks at the grill. Many of the bunkers and the practice putting greens take the unmistakable shape of Mickey Mouse's ears, but that does not prevent it being a challenging championship-level course, landscaped by experienced Californian architects. Information desks at City Hall inside the park (tel. 6474 3000) and in the hotels will tell you about bookings.

Tennis

Open-air hard courts are available at Hotel New York (100F per hour) and at Camp Davy Crockett (50F per hour). You can

Mickey and Goofy in suitably sporting attire at Golf Euro Disney.

buy tennis equipment from the Team Mickey shop at Festival Disney.

Swimming

You will find heated indoor pools at Disneyland Hotel, Hotel New York, the Newport Bay Club, the Sequoia Lodge and Camp Davy Crockett. In keeping with the hotel's National Parks-style décor, the Sequoia's pool comes specially landscaped in its own separate lodge. The big one at Camp Davy Crockett has water slides, a 'river', a waterfall and a children's pool. The Hotel New York and Newport Bay Club both have additional outdoor pools. If you've forgotten your costume, you can buy swim- and beachwear at Festival Disney's Surf Shop.

Boating

On the resort's Lake Buena Vista (an artificial lake, filtered every ten days) you can rent little Toobies – miniature motor boats built for two – for 50F per half hour.

Paddling Indian canoes down the Rivers of the Far West.

Skating

If you're a skating enthusiast you can try out your figures-of-eight or upright spins on the major sporting attraction at Hotel New York: the **Rockefeller Plaza ice rink**. It's framed by skyscrapers, just like the rink back in Manhattan, and is open throughout the winter. The charge for a two-hour session is 60F per adult, 50F per child and 40F per person in a group. There is a 15F reduction if you use your own skates.

Croquet

When you get back from tea with Alice, the March Hare, Mad Hatter and Dormouse, why not try your hand at that most vicious of genteel sports, favoured by British vicars, squires, ladies and their brutal children. The hoops, hammers and balls await you on the lawn at the Newport Bay Club.

Health Clubs

The Disneyland Hotel, Hotel New York, Newport Bay Club and Sequoia Lodge all have gyms where you can work out. Each one has aerobics and exercise equipment, jacuzzi, massage, sauna, solarium and steam rooms. Length-of-stay membership can be taken out at any of the health clubs for 100F, otherwise it costs 50F per visit. The solarium costs 100F for 30 minutes and a massage session is 200F for 30 minutes.

Cycling, Jogging and Pony Rides

Woodland trails have been laid out around Camp Davy Crockett for cycling, jogging and nature enthusiasts. The camp offers 24-hour bicycle rental (in the same barn as the golf carts) at 35F for adults and 25F for children. Children can ride ponies at Davy's Farm (10F per ride).

Field Sports

Sports fields at Camp Davy Crockett are available for **football**, **basketball** and **volleyball.** Alternatively, if you find all that rather too strenuous, you can try a little lazy Mediterranean **pétanque** instead.

Children's Playgrounds

For children who prefer to invent their own games, themed playgrounds have been provided at the Newport Bay Club, Sequoia Lodge, Hotel Cheyenne (special fun at Fort Apache and The Corral among Indian tepees and pioneer wagons) and Camp Davy Crockett.

Electronic Games

Test your reflexes in the games rooms and arcades to be found in all the resort hotels and Camp Davy Crockett.

Entertainment

Never forget that the Euro Disney Resort is above all a showbiz affair. Quite apart from the rides, there is always some sideshow going on: parades, plays, street antics, singers or fireworks displays.

Outside the park itself there are more shows and music at the hotels and, above all, at Festival Disney, south of the RER/TGV railway station.

Buffalo Bill's Wild West Show

Staged outside the theme park at Festival Disney, this is a whole

One of the star attractions of the spectacular Main Street Electrical Parade.

evening's entertainment. For 300 francs (200 francs for 3–11-year-olds, 1992 prices), you get the show, a hearty Western-style meal and a straw cowboy hat. And what a show! Buffalo Bill, Annie Oakley (of *Annie Get Your Gun* fame) and Sitting Bull join forces with cowboys, Indians (genuine Apaches and Sioux), rodeo clowns (authentic buffoons) and actors for a marvellous demonstration of the old arts, skills and music of the Wild West. For many, though, the real stars are the livestock – 11 bison, 37 horses (quarter horses, Appaloosas and pinto ponies), 12 longhorn cattle, and a great grey Brahma bull.

While at Festival Disney, you can continue the cowboy atmosphere with live music at **Billy Bob's Country Western Saloon** or go disco-dancing at **Hurricane's**, a night club in the style of Key West, Florida.

Hotel Nightlife

All the Euro Disney hotels have some form of live entertainment in their themed restaurants, bars or cocktail lounges. At the Disneyland Hotel, jazz and popular music are played at the **Main Street Lounge** overlooking the theme park. Just like the famous Manhattan nightspot, the **Rainbow Room** at the Hotel New York has Big Band music for its dinner-dance.

Cooler piano music prevails inside the Newport Bay Club at **Fisherman's Wharf**, with its cruise-liner décor and panoramic views over the lake, and in the **Redwood Bar** of the Sequoia Lodge.

At Hotel Cheyenne you have the choice between Country and Western music in the **Red Garter Saloon** and dancing at the **Yellow Rose Dance Hall**.

Euro Disneyland Parades

There are parades each day, but the two most spectacular, one by day, the other at night, make their way from outside the pavilion of It's a Small World, through Fantasyland, past the Castle and around the Discoveryland side of Central Plaza to Main Street, USA.

For the best overall view of the parades, go to Central Plaza or watch from Main Street itself.

La Parade Disney, as the daily parade is known, is a marvellously colourful array of a dozen floats bearing popular Disney characters through the park: Sleeping Beauty, the Castle Dragon, Pinocchio, Snow White and the Seven Dwarfs, Cinderella, Dumbo, Peter Pan, the animals from *The Jungle Book*, Benny the Cab and one of the most recent heroines, the Little Mermaid. They are all accompanied, of course, by music taken from the films that made them famous.

The night-time **Main Street Electrical Parade** imported from Florida is even more extravagant: 700,000 lights illuminate 22 glittering floats, trains, planes, fairy coaches, racing cars, all sparkling in the night and animated by Mickey, Minnie, Goofy, Donald and a cast of 125 performers. The Electrical Parade is followed by **81**

an equally spectacular **Fireworks Show**.

More casual are the **C'est Magique** romp-arounds, staged at the Fantasy Festival Stage throughout the day by 12 dancing Kids of the Kingdom and 11 Disney characters. Even without following it, you may catch a piece of this wherever you happen to be in Fantasyland. Mickey kicks off the show on Main Street, USA. Goofy picks it up in Frontierland where, dressed as a cowboy, he **82** has a fight with 'Wild Indian'

Watch Buffalo Bill's Wild West Show at Festival Disney or pose with Goofy in Frontierland.

chipmunks Chip and Dale. Meanwhile, Miss Minnie is dancing the cancan over at the Lucky Nugget Saloon. The monkeys play Dixie in Adventureland and more modern music has the dancers rocking in Discoveryland. Dressed as a fairy prince and princess, Mickey and Minnie perform the finale with other Disney characters.

Lucky Nugget Saloon

Situated just inside the entrance of Frontierland, this comfortable saloon is designed to look like a luxury establishment during San Francisco's Gold Rush years: it's fitted out with golden oak furniture, brass chandeliers and red velvet curtains with tassels. Notice the splendid mahogany saloon bar with brass fittings, and the great 'Lucky Nugget' of gold in the bell-jar. Over an appropriately robust dinner (see p.90), you can watch a boisterous 30-minute dance-hall revue, complete with cancan girls. The place is run by Diamond Lil, who sings 'A Good Man is Hard to Find'. The man she does find is Parisian lover Pierre Paradis, whose theme song is 'They Go Wild, Simply Wild Over Me'. An enthralling performance of the gripping melodrama, *The Perils of Little Nell* (complete with heroine being rescued from railway tracks), is followed by the grand finale of frilly cancan. *Magnifique!*

Musicians and Street Entertainers

The creators of the Euro Disney Resort understand that queuing is usually boring, and that queuing at the Euro Disneyland Park in one place or another is unavoidable. So they have decided to banish the boredom by providing a little entertainment. There are a couple of dozen street performers to keep you amused as you wander around the park.

The rousing oom-paah-pah on Main Street, USA is provided by the 19 talented musicians of the grand **Euro Disneyland Band**, who also perform at the castle stage and in La Parade Disney (the daytime parade). When it is not singing sweet serenades on its home turf at the Harmony Barber Shop, the **Barber Shop Quartet** rides about on the trolley or on its bicycle built for four. You'll find **Casey's Ragtime Piano and Banjo** act at Casey's Corner, and the **Keystone Kops**, a comic saxophone quintet, creating havoc on Main Street.

In Frontierland, up on the roof of the Lucky Nugget saloon, you may spot a farcical shoot-out between **The Gunfighters**, while **The Card Shark** tricks people in the queue waiting outside Phantom Manor. Country and Western music is the speciality of **The Cowhand Band** quartet playing at the Cowboy Cookout Barbecue, while the **Mariachis** play authentic Mexican music at the Fuente del Oro Restaurante.

In Adventureland there is a lively Caribbean steel band, **The Blue Lagoon Trio**, on hand to entertain guests at the restaurant of the same name. The Explorers Club is host to the extraordinary **Dr Livingstone**, a bizarre ukulele-playing big-game hunter. Meanwhile the **African Tam-Tams** play near the exotic restaurant, Aux Epices Enchantées.

In Fantasyland **The Jesters** do an acrobatic juggling act in the courtyard of Le Château de la Belle au Bois Dormant (Sleeping Beauty's Castle), while their buddy, the **Troubador**, plays his lute at the Auberge de Cendrillon.

Discoveryland's brass band, **Les Voyageurs**, performs contemporary music by Stravinsky, Aaron Copeland and *Star Wars* composer John Williams. **The Robomimes** are roller-skating robots entertaining the queues at Videopolis, Star Tours and CinéMagique. And crazy flying machines, known as 'Flights of Fantasy', create mayhem in the streets of Discoveryland when they aren't pedalling in time with the daytime parade.

Fiddling in Frontierland – one of several Disney sideshows.

Le Théâtre du Château

On the castle stage, dancers and characters perform *Sleeping Beauty* as a mini-musical comedy with a stage-set resembling a children's pop-up book. Special effects include a real white stallion leaping on to the stage, and the music is by Tchaikovsky.

Videopolis

The daytime entertainment at Discoveryland's futuristic showplace (see p.71) is the hyper-energetic journey of 20 rock 'n' roll dancers led by four teenage 'Explorers'. Lasers, lights and mind-shaking music take you through the cosmos, beneath the sea and back to earth.

Euro Disney Resort Accommodation

South of the theme park are six Disney hotels – two luxury, two first class and two moderate – providing 5,200 rooms, most capable of accommodating a family of four. There is a spacious country site for 181 camping and caravan spaces and 414 bungalows (each sleeping a family of 4–6). Like the lands inside Euro Disneyland, each hotel has a 'theme' – this time evoking a region of the United States, not only in its architecture and landscaping but also in the food offered in the hotel restaurants (see pp.93–5).

Amenities

All the hotels have rooms for disabled guests and designated non-smoking rooms. Hotel rooms and camp cabins are equipped with direct-dial telephones and television receiving closed-circuit films and international channels. The hotels offer baby-sitting services. Shuttle-bus transportation is available to the theme park and the RER/TGV station from the hotels and Camp Davy Crockett.

Disneyland Hotel

The resort's luxury flagship hotel is at the theme park entrance. Its pink and white design recalls the style of Florida and California resort hotels in the first half of this century. Some of the 500 rooms, including 21 suites, offer a panoramic view of Euro Disneyland.

Hotel New York

Situated near Festival Disney and the RER/TGV station, this luxury hotel with convention facilities recalls Manhattan's midtown skyscrapers, with lower wings of East Side brownstones. Its 574 Art Déco rooms include 36 suites. The hotel's centrepiece is its Rockefeller Plaza skating rink.

Newport Bay Club

At the other end of Lake Buena Vista from the Hotel New York, this first-class hotel is in the grand style of the New England seaside resorts of the early 1900s. It has a yacht club feel, and rocking chairs on the verandah look out over the croquet field. It boasts 1,098 rooms, including 15 suites, all with a nautical decor.

Sequoia Lodge

Here the atmosphere is reminiscent of the American National Parks lodges – a first-class timber and stone hotel complex grouped in a wooded setting around rivers leading from Lake Buena Vista. There arc 1,011 rooms decorated like hunting lodges, including 14 suites in riverside lodges. The indoor swimming pool here is landscaped in its own lodge.

Hotel Cheyenne

This hotel is moderately priced, as befits the Western frontier town which its buildings recall – a saloon for the adults, a fort and Indian village for children to play in. Fourteen buildings along Desperado Street on one side and the Rio Grande river on the other house 1,000 Wild West rooms with bunk beds for the children.

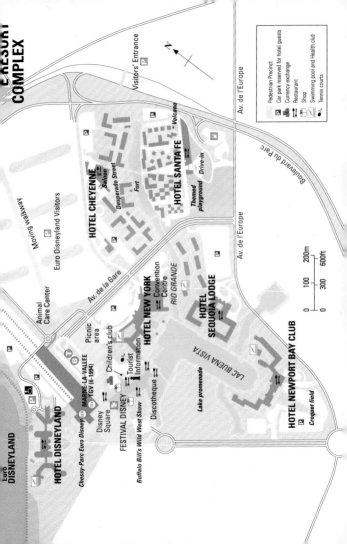

EURO DISNEY RESORT COMPLEX

euro
DISNEYLAND

HOTEL DISNEYLAND

Chessy-Parc Euro Disney · MARNE-LA-VALLEE TGV (6·1994)

Animal Care Center

Moving walkway

Euro Disneyland Visitors

Visitors' Entrance

Disney Square

FESTIVAL DISNEY

Buffalo Bill's Wild West Show

Picnic area

Children's club

Tourist Information

Discotheque

Av. de la Gare

HOTEL CHEYENNE

Saloon

Desperado Street

Fort

HOTEL SANTA FE

Volcano

Themed playground

Drive-in

HOTEL NEW YORK

Convention Centre

RIO GRANDE

HOTEL SEQUOIA LODGE

LAC BUENA VISTA

Lake promenade

HOTEL NEWPORT BAY CLUB

Croquet field

Boulevard du Parc

Av. de l'Europe

Av. de l'Europe

N

Pedestrian Precinct
Car park reserved for hotel guests
Currency exchange
Restaurant
Shop
Swimming pool and Health club
Tennis courts

| 0 | 100 | 200m |
| 0 | 300 | 600ft |

The luxurious Disneyland Hotel has unique views over the theme park.

Hotel Santa Fe

This is situated south of the Rio Grande, surrounded by symbols of the American South West. It is a moderately priced hotel-village of New Mexico inspiration – 1,000 rooms in 42 attractive, adobe-style houses.

Camp Davy Crockett

The atmosphere here is that of a pioneering stockaded Western fort. Camp Davy Crockett is set in a forest covering 56 hectares (138 acres) – the same size as the theme park itself. However, the pioneers didn't have it this good: the 414 log cabins have fully equipped kitchens, bedroom with bathroom en suite, living room, TV, telephone, and daily house-keeping services. Outside each cabin is a picnic area and barbecue. There are also 181 campsites for tents or caravans, with running water, picnic tables, electrical hook-ups and toilet facilities. (See pp.76–9, for Camp Davy Crockett's other outdoor assets.)

Reservations

In the UK you can telephone 071 753 2900 for information or reservations. Or contact the Central Reservations Office, BP 105, 77777 Marne-la-Vallée Cedex 4, France; tel. (33 1) 4941 4910; fax (33 1) 4930 7100 or 4930 7170. Prices vary according to length of stay and other conditions but compare well with rates in Paris for the categories given here: luxury, first class and moderate.

Eating Out

You won't go hungry at the Euro Disney Resort. The opportunities for different kinds of meals, from quick snacks to elegant full-course dinners, are legion. In the past, theme parks in general were accused by the health-conscious of breeding a generation of obese and pimply monsters by providing nothing but fatty and sugary fast food. The fare at Euro Disneyland is much more balanced. There are *good* hamburgers, great pizza, and ice-cream for which true connoisseurs consider it sufficient simply to say that it is genuine American. There are also plenty of salads, fresh vegetables and a whole host of savoury dishes from all over the world. Discover unimagined facets of American cuisine, as well as cooking from the Middle East, Africa, Thailand, India, China, Latin America and the Caribbean. And in the hands of Disney film-makers the décor is half the fun. Nobody expects to find a gourmet paradise in a theme park, but this is a five-star theme park.

After an eventful day in the theme park, relax with a drink in one of the resort's hospitable bars.

Below is a guide to the restaurants throughout the park, land by land, plus a survey of the restaurants available at the hotels and Festival Disney.

Main Street, USA

The choice here is proudly classical American.

Walt's – an American Restaurant – next to Liberty Court, its table service offers regional American dishes – fish, steaks and roast chicken – in an old-fashioned atmosphere

Victoria's Home-Style Cooking – on the north-east block opposite Walt's, this restaurant offers pot pies as its speciality, served at the counter along with salads. There is also a selection of desserts, starring freshly baked apple pie. In the same building try the **Cookie Kitchen** for real American cookies and the **Cable Car Bake Shop** for pastries, cakes and pies.

Plaza Gardens Restaurant – the park's biggest buffet-service restaurant serves soups, salads, roast chicken and grills in a Victorian garden setting.

Market House Deli – this serves freshly made sandwiches at the counter: hot turkey, pastrami, corned beef, chicken salad and tuna. The New York-style cheesecake is a must.

Casey's Corner – on the same block as the deli, this sells hot dogs, hottest chilli and soft drinks in a baseball setting named after the fictional title character of the poem, 'Casey at the Bat', by Ernest L. Thayer. The piano player does 'Take Me Out To The Ball Game'.

The Coffee Grinder – near Casey's Corner, this is the place to go for coffee and croissants.

The Gibson Girl Ice Cream Parlour and **The Ice Cream Company** – this is where the unsuspecting should try the sinfully delicious malted milkshakes and the Rocky Road ice-cream, which belongs in any gastronomic Hall of Fame.

Frontierland

Sample the food that won the West.

The Lucky Nugget Saloon – just inside the Fort Comstock entrance. With Diamond Lil as hostess (see p.83), you get great roast beef (they call it 'prime rib' here), chicken and barbecued spare ribs at the evening show, salads for lunch and pie in the afternoon.

Silver Spur Steakhouse – in this high-class joint opposite the Thunder Mesa riverboat landing you can watch your steak or other grill being prepared. Dine off the ranchers' finest china, drink French wines in crystal goblets, and mind you don't stain the white table linen.

Last Chance Café – with 'Wanted' posters on the wall of

It's worth working up a healthy appetite for the Cowboy Cookout Barbecue.

this bandits' hideout, count yourself lucky to get good hamburgers, hot dogs and soft drinks.

Cowboy Cookout Barbecue – in a barn adjacent to Cottonwood Creek Ranch, eat spare ribs, chicken and other barbecue fare with live Country and Western or bluegrass music.

Fuente del Oro Restaurante – in adobe-style architecture on

the border with Adventureland, you can enjoy Tex-Mex *tortillas, tacos, enchiladas, frijoles, fajitas* and spicy *salsa,* with live mariachi music thrown in.

Adventureland

Here you will find the fragrance and spices of faraway lands.

Aux Epices Enchantées – outside the Bazar facing La Cabane des Robinson, this place might serve Chinese, Thai, Japanese or Moroccan cuisine, but the décor is African – a high-pitched thatched roof, clay and mud walls with native carvings, masks and folk art in the interior. Outdoor meals are served under brightly coloured African umbrellas. Specialities include kebabs of chicken, pork, beef and prawn, stir-fried vegetables, spring rolls, tropical fruit pies and coconut ice-cream.

Café de la Brousse – this atmospheric counter-service restaurant is set in palm-frond huts with grass-thatching, overlooking Adventure Isle, and serves *kefta pita* (meatballs in pita bread), mint tea and soft drinks.

Explorers Club – this is in the heart of Adventureland, with a delightful tropical design of white wood panels, red corrugated metal roofs and a verandah

overlooking waterfalls. Inside, the jungle: hunting trophies, safari paraphernalia, Polynesian masks, a canoe, an anchor ... and a giant Banyan tree complete with birds. It's the perfect setting for fine seafood, poultry and wild game.

Blue Lagoon Restaurant – this is inside Pirates of the Caribbean, and you can choose from an exciting menu which includes exotic soups, steaks or seafood, fish in banana leaf with mango, and tropical drinks. All of this amid palm trees, a white sand beach, a moonlit sky, and the musical accompaniment of a West Indian steel band.

Captain Hook's Galley – this offers cookies and other light snacks as part of the Adventure Isle attraction.

Fantasyland

The food in Fantasyland has an unmistakable touch of fairytale whimsy.

Auberge de Cendrillon – the French château design, with its décor fit for a princess, takes you inside to the scene of Cinderella receiving her ballgown and pumpkin-turned-glass coach in a banquet hall glowing with pixie dust. All is pinks and blues. Fountains, statues, hand-woven tapestries from Aubusson, and romantic curtained booths set the mood. The food? Classical French fare, with 'mocktails' (delicious non-alcoholic cocktails) for the children, who may cause a scene if you don't get them a Cinderella Coach dessert.

Au Chalet de la Marionnette – situated next to the Pinocchio attraction, this Alpine-style cottage has counter-service for Italian sausages, sandwiches and strudels.

Toad Hall Restaurant – beside Peter Pan's Flight, this half-timbered English country manor celebrates characters from Kenneth Grahame's *The Wind in the Willows*. Traditional English fare prevails: fish and chips, steak and kidney pie and trifle.

Pizzeria Bella Notte – closer to It's a Small World, the pizzas and pasta are served in a décor inspired by the romantic Venetian trattoria in *Lady and the Tramp*. Continue the Italian theme with an ice-cream next door at **Fantasia Gelati**.

March Hare Refreshments – beside Alice's Curious Labyrinth, this unabashedly eccentric house (note the sagging windows) serves 'unbirthday' cakes and other snacks, teas and coffee.

The Old Mill – in a patio garden between the maze and It's a Small World, this Dutch windmill serves yoghurt, desserts, apple cake and fruit tarts.

Discoveryland

This is the future so the service is particularly fast – almost out of this world, in fact.

Café des Visionnaires – set just behind Le Visionarium, this is the place for hungry globe-trotters to find huge salads and hot dishes.

Café Hypérion – under the airship in Videopolis, with counter service for hamburgers, sandwiches, pizzas, pasta and salads, which can be enjoyed while watching the entertainment in the adjoining amphitheatre.

The Hotels

The cuisine follows the regional themes of the hotels, offering table, buffet and counter service.

Disneyland Hotel – there is all-American elegance, but an easy-going atmosphere, at the **California Grill**; traditional American food is served buffet-style at **Inventions**; overlooking Disney Square, **Café Fantasia** takes its décor from Mickey's musical classic.

Hotel New York – 30s-style dinner-dance with Big Band music at the **Rainbow Room** and all-day dining at the **Park Side Diner**.

Newport Bay Club – excellent New England-style seafood **93**

Breakfast with Minnie

At Disneyland Hotel's Inventions buffet-restaurant and Hotel New York's Rainbow Room, you can book a special breakfast with costumed characters from the theme park. Disney characters join you at your table for a photo opportunity that is the envy even of American Presidents. Ask at the hotel information desk about reservations for these 'Character Breakfasts'.

and natural farm produce at the **Cape Cod**; shellfish and the spectacular Rhode Island 'Clambake' at the **Yacht Club**.

Sequoia Lodge – rôtisserie of marinated meats and poultry at the **Hunter's Grill** and barbecued chicken, beef and ribs at the **Beaver Creek Tavern.**

Hotel Cheyenne – Texas-style barbecue and hickory-flavoured meats and poultry at the **Chuckwagon Café.**

Hotel Santa Fe – Tex-Mex cuisine is served at **La Cantina**.

A 'Character Breakfast' (left) in a Disney hotel is the ultimate holiday treat.

Camp Davy Crockett – when you are not cooking for yourself in your cabin or on the campsite (you can buy a variety of groceries from the **Alamo Trading Post**), hearty American home-style cooking is available at **Crockett's Tavern**, a self-service restaurant.

Festival Disney

There are restaurants for all tastes inside the entertainment complex: an oyster bar at **Key West Seafood**, designed like a Floridian crab shack; top-quality beef and fine wines at the elegant **Steakhouse**; steaks and pizza at the **Los Angeles Bar & Grill**; all-day meals at the 50s-style **Annette's Diner**; fast-food at **Champion's Sports Bar**; and delicatessen food – lox and bagels, hot pastrami and salt beef sandwiches – at **Carnegie's Deli**. **95**

Excursions

The Euro Disney Resort is within easy reach of Paris and the chief cultural landmarks of the region. For visitors staying three days or longer it is worth taking time to explore the capital or the countryside. Here is a brief guide to the main sights you may see.

Paris

More than most national capitals, Paris dictates the country's tastes and lifestyle. The city and its people share a boundless self-confidence that exudes from every stone in its monuments and museums, bistros and boutiques, from every chestnut tree along its avenues and boulevards, from every street urchin, mannequin, butcher and baker, from every irate motorist and every charming maître d'hôtel.

Notre-Dame Cathedral

The site of the cathedral has had religious significance for at least 2,000 years. In Roman times a temple to Jupiter stood here, followed in the 4th century by Paris's first Christian church, Saint-Etienne. To replace ruins left by Norman invaders, Bishop Maurice de Sully ordered the present cathedral to be constructed in 1163. The main part of Notre-Dame took 167 years to complete and, in its transition from Romanesque to Gothic, it has been called a perfect expression of medieval architecture.

Built to inspire awe, Notre-Dame remains impressive, truly the nation's parish church. It has witnessed, in 1239, Louis IX walking barefoot with his holy relic, Christ's crown of thorns; in 1430 the humiliation of having Henry VI of England crowned King of France; in 1594 the Catholic mass that sealed the conversion of Protestant Henri IV; in 1804 Napoleon's coronation; and, in more recent times, the state funerals of war heroes such as Foch, Joffre and de Gaulle.

In the grandiose façade, notice the magnificent **rose window** encircling a statue of the Virgin Mary and Child. Across the top of the three doorways the statues in the **Galerie des Rois** represent the 28 kings of Judah and Israel – replicas, since the originals were destroyed by French revolutionaries mistaking them for the kings of France.

The only original bell left is in the South Tower, especially pure in tone because of the gold and silver mixed with its bronze. Like the others, it is operated not by a hunchback but by an electric system installed in 1953.

Notre-Dame Cathedral – superb setting for some of the most dramatic scenes in French history.

The Louvre

The royal palace that is now the biggest museum in the world has been the plaything of France's rulers from King Philippe Auguste, who built the original fortress in 1190, to President François Mitterrand, who commissioned the great glass pyramid in the Cour Napoléon. It is impossible to see more than a very few of the treasures (250,000 in the most recent inventory), so here is a brief selection:

Greek – the winged but headless *Victory of Samothrace* and the beautifully proportioned *Venus de Milo*.

Italian – Leonardo da Vinci's famous *Mona Lisa*, but also his sublime *Virgin of the Rocks;* Titian's voluptuous *Woman at her Toilet*, and Caravaggio's astonishing *Death of the Virgin*.

French – Watteau's melancholy *Gilles*, Géricault's

dramatic and macabre *Raft of the Medusa*, and Delacroix's triumphant *Liberty Guiding the People*.

Dutch and Flemish – Rembrandt's cheerful *Self-Portrait with a Toque* and his beloved *Hendrickje Stoffels;* Van Dyck's dignified *Charles I,* Rubens' tenderly personal *Helena Fourment* and Jordaens' *Four Evangelists* as diligent Dutchmen.

German – Dürer's gripping *Self-Portrait* and Holbein's cool *Erasmus*.

Spanish – the wonderfully ugly portrait of *Queen Marianna of Austria* by Velázquez, and El Greco's powerful *Christ on the Cross*.

English – Gainsborough's exquisite *Conversation in a Park* and Turner's almost abstract *Landscape with River and Bay*.

Musée d'Orsay

The 19th-century Orsay railway station has been transformed into a magnificent museum. It celebrates France's tremendous creativity from 1848–1914, not only in painting, sculpture, architecture and industrial design, but also in advertising, newspapers, book publishing, photography and the early years of the cinema. Painting is highlighted by the great **Impressionists** and **Post-Impressionists**, Monet, Manet, Renoir, Cézanne, Van Gogh and Gauguin, but there are also masterpieces by Courbet and by the Americans James Whistler and Winslow Homer, both of whom worked in Paris.

Champs-Elysées

This remains the city's most glamorous avenue. With chestnut trees along its entire length, it stretches in a perfect straight line from the **Arc de Triomphe**, Napoleon's gigantic triumphal arch, to **Place de la Concorde**, where the guillotine operated during the French Revolution. As you walk down, the first two thirds of the avenue are devoted to cinemas, shops and café terraces. You'll find the best vantage points for that favourite Parisian pastime of people-watching between Avenue George V and Rue Lincoln on the 'shady' side and at the Rue du Colisée on the 'sunny' side. An interesting theory of Champs-Elysées veterans holds that people look more relaxed and attractive when walking downhill, so you can ignore the ones going up.

The Seine

The river is by far the best place from which to take the measure of the city. Its mixture of grandeur and intimacy is the very essence of Paris. The great monuments – the Eiffel Tower, the

National Assembly, the Louvre and Notre-Dame – all take on a more enchanting, dreamlike quality from the river. Walt Disney would have taken the boat.

Four bridges stand out: the **Pont Alexandre III**, beloved of lovers, is undoubtedly the most kitschily romantic of all, with its Belle Epoque lanterns and melodramatic statues of Fame and Pegasus. **Pont de la Concorde** is truly the bridge of the French Revolution. Completed in 1790, its support structure used stone from the demolished Bastille prison. **Pont des Arts** is a delightful new wooden structure with flower beds in the middle, and is popular for picnics. **Pont-Neuf** (*neuf* means 'new') is in fact Paris's oldest standing bridge, completed by Henri IV in 1606 – that's him on horseback in the middle. It used to be a favourite spot for street-singers, pickpockets, charlatans, amateur dentists, professional ladies and, above all, *bouquinistes* selling old books and pamphlets out of boxes. Established booksellers on the adjacent Ile de la Cité were enraged and drove them off to the banks of the Seine, where they've been ever since.

Take the lift up the Eiffel Tower for the best possible view of France.

Eiffel Tower

There are monuments and there is the Eiffel Tower. Some celebrate heroes, commemorate victories, honour kings and saints. The *Tour Eiffel* is a monument for its own sake, a proud gesture to the world, a witty structure making aesthetics irrelevant. Its construction for the World's Fair of 1889 was an astounding engineering feat – 15,000 pieces of metal joined together by 2,500,000

rivets soaring 300 m (984 ft) into the air on a base covering only 130 sq m (1,400 sq ft).

Like many other World's Fair exhibits, the Eiffel Tower was slated for destruction, but nobody had the heart to do it, despite the hostility of contemporary leaders of taste. Guy de Maupassant signed a manifesto against 'this vertiginously ridiculous tower', and the poet Verlaine rerouted his journey around Paris to avoid seeing it (difficult now, almost impossible then). Today, everyone seems to love it. It has a splendid inner illumination at night, a popular brasserie on the first platform, and an elegant gourmet restaurant on the second. From the top, the view extends over 60 km (40 miles) on a pollution-free day.

Versailles

It's best to go round the palace in the morning and the gardens in the afternoon. There can be a lot of walking, so take good shoes.

The Palace

To understand King Louis XIV, take a long, hard look at his palace. Never did a piece of architecture more exactly express its builder's personality than the Château of Versailles – extravagant, pompous, dazzling,

formidable, vainglorious. Like the sun with which the King identified, the palace became the centre of his 17th-century universe, proclaiming his grandeur in a sprawling edifice of stone and brick, marble, gilt and crystal. This is not Fantasyland.

The palace has been beautifully restored since World War I with private contributions, most notably from J.D. Rockefeller. Wherever original furnishings are missing, the finest equivalents have been installed.

After crossing the vast, intimidating Cour des Ministres past the imperious statue of Louis XIV, the self-guided tour begins more reassuringly at the intimate little **Royal Chapel**. This gem of High Baroque presents a harmonious décor of white marble with gilded altar and balustrades. You get the king's-eye-view down into the nave where the courtiers used to worship.

In the **Grands Appartements** named after Greek gods and goddesses, courtiers were received three times a week, Monday, Wednesday and Thursday. The **Salon de Diane** was a billiard room – not many people could

Classical gardens complement the formal splendour of Versailles.

beat the King. The table has gone, but Bernini has left a superb bust of the champion at 27 years of age. The **Salon d'Apollon**, with the Sun King in his chariot portrayed on the ceiling and pictorial references to Alexander the Great and Augustus Caesar, was of course his throne room.

The most astounding of these royal apartments is the glittering **Galerie des Glaces**, 73 m (240 ft) long, built to catch every ray of the setting sun in the tall arched panels of mirrors. After victory over the French in 1871, Germany's Emperor Wilhelm I was crowned here, but the French took their revenge by using it for the treaty-signing which sealed Germany's humiliation in World War I.

The Gardens

If English and Japanese gardens attempt to enhance nature by 'tidying it up' while imitating a 'natural' landscape, the classical French garden, of which Versailles presents the supreme example, quite deliberately imposes a formal pattern. The paths and avenues of trees and statuary trace an intricate geometry among the flowerbeds, ponds and fountain basins.

On your way through the grounds, look back at the changing perspectives of the palace.

Directly beyond the western terrace is the Axe du Soleil (Path of the Sun) leading down to the **Bassin d'Apollon**. Adorned with classical sculptures of Greek mythology, this and the great **Bassin de Neptune** and **Bassin du Dragon** in the north-east corner were centrepieces for the royal garden parties. Beyond the Bassin d'Apollon, is the **Grand Canal** on which the King kept his Venetian gondolas.

North west of the château, the less pretentious **Grand Trianon** palace was the home of Louis XIV's mistress, Madame de Maintenon.

The **Petit Trianon**, where Marie-Antoinette tried to hide from that nasty Revolution, has the allure of a doll's house when compared with the rest of Versailles. Its gardens, with ponds, mounds and shady woods, are English in style. The childlike playfulness of the doomed queen's hideaway is reinforced by her **Hameau**, a hamlet of thatched cottages where she and her retinue pretended to be milkmaids and farmhands, a veritable 18th-century theme park.

Vaux-le-Vicomte and Fontainebleau

Equally impressive in their way, but more human and

'manageable' than Versailles in their dimensions, these two châteaux make an interesting contrast in Renaissance and Baroque styles.

Vaux-le-Vicomte

State financier Nicolas Fouquet's grandiose 17th-century residence offers an exquisite object-lesson in the humiliation of the high and mighty. Following in the footsteps of Cardinals Richelieu and Mazarin, Fouquet amassed a huge fortune from his job with the motto *Quo non ascendem?* ('What heights can I not scale?'). Louis XIV showed him. When the King was invited for dinner in 1661 he threw a temper tantrum at the extravagance of the reception and the opulence of the place. He tossed Fouquet in jail and appropriated his architect Louis Le Vau, painter-decorator Charles Le Brun and landscape-architect André Le Nôtre to go off and build Versailles.

As you can see by the unfinished splendour of the rotunda's **Grand Salon**, Le Brun had to leave in a hurry. But in Le Nôtre's **gardens** you can still appreciate the wonderful perspectives and surprise effects of the pools and canals.

Fontainebleau

The majestic **Forest of Fontainebleau** covers 25,000 hectares (over 60,000 acres) of oak, beech, silver birch, pine, chestnut and hornbeam. On the western outskirts is the village of **Barbizon**, home of many important 19th-century landscape painters, most notably Corot, Millet and Théodore Rousseau.

Favoured for hunting by Kings François I and Henri IV, the palace of Fontainebleau in the middle of the forest is an elegant monument to their Renaissance tastes. Napoleon cherished it as a place for reflection, and it was there that he abdicated in 1814 to go into his first exile on the Isle of Elba.

Allegorical paintings in the **Galerie de François I** bear testimony to the king's preoccupation with war and death, and also to the sanctity of kingship. **Napoleon's apartments** are still decorated with the furnishings of his empire. A Napoleonic museum has been installed in the Louis XV wing.

Reims and the Champagne Country

Champagne is the wine of kings and it was in Reims cathedral that the kings of France were anointed and crowned – Hugues Capet, the first king of France, in 987 and Charles X, the last of the Bourbons, in 1825.

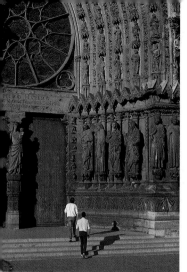

yond the high altar is the **Chagall chapel** in which the Russian artist connects his Jewish origins to the Christian religion with a window showing Abraham and Jesus.

The Champagne Vineyards

There are only 23,000 hectares (57,000 acres) of true Champagne vineyards – 1.5% of the national total – and their grapes alone, black and white, are authorized to go into a Champagne bottle. The light, fresh note is provided by the white chardonnay grapes growing south of **Epernay** in the vineyards known as **Côte des blancs**. The black pinot noir grapes on the **Montagne de Reims** add body, and pinot meunier west of Epernay add a dash of fruitiness. You'll find these grapes all over the wine-growing world, but only the Champagne region has that special chalky soil, not only for the vineyards, but also for the vaults of the gallery cellars you will visit, maintaining a constant temperature of 10.5°C (51°F) during the months that turn wine into champagne.

Cheers!

Reims Cathedral

The magnificently proportioned 13th-century cathedral was badly damaged by fire in World War I, but it has been well restored and remains one of the country's great Gothic edifices. On the lovely buff stone façade, it's worth using a pair of binoculars to study the rich sculpture of the Gallery of Kings high above the windows. In the interior, look for the **stained-glass rose window** above the western entrance, illustrating the life of the Virgin Mary. In the north arm of the transept, another fine window depicts the Creation. Directly be-

BLUEPRINT for a Perfect Trip

How to Get There

Getting to the Euro Disney Resort from Paris, the airports or the provinces is being simplified by the new RER and future TGV express rail links and new stretches of *autoroute* (motorway) leading right to the site.

BY AIR

Scheduled flights

Paris is served by two international airports, Roissy-Charles-de-Gaulle and Orly (see also p.110). The average journey time between Paris and London is 1 hour, New York 7 hours (less than 4 by Concorde), Toronto 9 hours, Johannesburg 14 hours, and Sydney and Auckland 24 hours.

Charter flights and package tours

From the UK and Eire: Most tour operators charter seats on scheduled flights at a reduced price as part of a package deal which could include two, three or four days' stay or longer. These holiday packages may involve a Euro Disney Resort Hotel, with excursions to Paris and other destinations in the region, or conversely a hotel in Paris or the Marne-la-Vallée area, with trips arranged to Euro Disneyland.

However, most visitors from the UK travel to France independently, either by booking directly with a ferry operator and taking the car, or signing up for inclusive holidays which offer fly-drive and touring arrangements.

From North America: ABC (Advance Booking Charters) provide air passage only (from New York, Chicago, Los Angeles and San Francisco to Paris), but OTC (One Stop Inclusive Tour Charter) package deals include airport transfers, hotel, some sightseeing and meals.

Your travel agent can inform you of special arrangements being made to include the Euro Disney Resort in packages that also involve wine-tasting tours and circuits around the Loire château country and other regions. These leave from over a dozen major American and Canadian cities, usually on a seasonal basis (April–October) and for periods of 1–3 weeks. You can also choose from fly-drive and fly-rail schemes.

From Australia, New Zealand and South Africa: Airlines and travel agents are including Euro Disneyland in their package deals. Contact them for details.

BY CAR

Coming from the English Channel, head for Paris on the A1 Autoroute, but turn off east after Roissy-Charles-de-Gaulle Airport on the A104 to the eastbound A4 at Marne-la-Vallée. Continue to the Parc Euro Disneyland exit, leading directly to the resort entrance.

BY BUS

Regular services operate from London to Paris (via Calais). Shuttle buses to the Euro Disney Resort run directly from Roissy-Charles-de-Gaulle and Orly airports.

BY RAIL

All the main lines converge on Paris. There is an excellent network of ultra-rapid express trains, TGVs (1st and 2nd class, advance booking obligatory, certain trains with supplement). Car sleeper trains *(trains autos couchettes)* are also available from all major towns.

The journey from London to Paris takes 6–11 hours by train. British and French railways offer London-to-Paris services with the possibility of overnight carriages from London. From Boulogne hoverport, the turbo-train to Paris (Gare du Nord) takes 2 hours 20 minutes.

Paris–Euro Disney Resort: the RER rapid transit service's eastbound Torcy line (A4) goes from five Paris stations (Etoile, Auber, Châtelet, Gare de Lyon and Nation) straight to the entrance of the Euro Disney Resort (station: Marne-la-Vallée–Chessy). You must purchase an RER ticket (Paris Métro tickets are not valid).

From June 1994 the TGV express from the provinces and other countries in Europe will stop right at the park entrance.

When to Go

The Paris region enjoys a mild Continental climate without extremes of hot and cold. Besides the obvious high-season periods like Easter, July and August and Christmas, you might note that French schools also take mid-term holidays in February and early November. If you are combining Euro Disneyland with Paris, the most pleasant seasons for the latter are spring and autumn. The following chart gives an idea of the average monthly temperatures for the region:

	J	F	M	A	M	J	J	A	S	O	N	D
°C	3	4	7	10	14	16	19	18	15	11	6	4
°F	37	39	45	50	57	61	66	64	59	52	43	3

Some Useful French Vocabulary

If you are having a meal outside the Euro Disney Resort and need some help with your 'restaurant French', here are a few tips:

To Help You Order...

Do you have a table?	**Avez-vous une table?**
Do you have a set-price menu?	**Avez vous un menu prix fixe?**
I'd like a/an/some ...	**J'aimerais ...**

beer	**une bière**	menu	**la carte**
bread	**du pain**	milk	**du lait**
butter	**du beurre**	mineral water	**de l'eau**
cheese	**du fromage**		**minérale**
coffee	**un café**	potatoes	**des pommes**
dessert	**un dessert**		**de terre**
egg	**un oeuf**	salad	**une salade**
fish	**du poisson**	sandwich	**un sandwich**
glass	**un verre**	soup	**de la soupe**
ice-cream	**une glace**	sugar	**du sucre**
lemon	**du citron**	tea	**du thé**
meat	**de la viande**	wine	**du vin**

... and Read the Menu

agneau	**lamb**	chou	**cabbage**
ail	**garlic**	chou-fleur	**cauliflower**
anchois	**anchovy**	concombre	**cucumber**
andouillette	**tripe sausage**	coquelet	**baby chicken**
artichaut	**artichoke**	coquille	**scallops**
asperges	**asparagus**	Saint-Jacques	
bar	**sea-bass**	côte, côtelette	**chop, cutlet**
bifteck	**steak**	crevettes	**shrimps**
blanquette de veau	**veal stew**	daurade	**sea-bream**
boeuf	**beef**	écrevisse	**crayfish**
caille	**quail**	épinards	**spinach**
canard, caneton	**duck, duckling**	flageolets	**dried beans**
cervelle	**brains**	foie	**liver**
champignons	**mushrooms**	fraises	**strawberries**

framboises	**raspberries**	pintade	**guinea fowl**
frites	**chips**	poire	**pear**
fruits de mer	**seafood**	poireaux	**leeks**
gigot (d'agneau)	**leg of lamb**	poisson	**fish**
haricots verts	**green beans**	pomme	**apple**
homard	**lobster**	porc	**pork**
huîtres	**oysters**	potage	**soup**
jambon	**ham**	poulet	**chicken**
langouste	**spiny lobster**	radis	**radishes**
langue	**tongue**	raisins	**grapes**
lapin	**rabbit**	ris de veau	**sweetbreads**
loup de mer	**sea-bass**	riz	**rice**
macédoine de fruits	**fruit salad**	rognons	**kidneys**
		rouget	**red mullet**
médaillon	**tenderloin**	saucisse/	**sausage/**
moules	**mussels**	saucisson	**dried sausage**
moutarde	**mustard**	saumon	**salmon**
mulet	**grey mullet**	sole	**sole**
navarin	**lamb stew**	thon	**tuna**
nouilles	**noodles**	truffes	**truffles**
oignons	**onions**	truite	**trout**
oseille	**sorrel**	veau	**veal**
petits pois	**peas**	volaille	**poultry**

An A–Z Summary
of Practical Information and Facts

> At Euro Disney, English is of course spoken everywhere, but for visitors staying in hotels outside the resort we have listed after many main entries an appropriate French translation (in the singular) and useful phrases.

A **AIRPORTS** *(aéroport)*. Paris is served by two main airports. **Roissy-Charles-de-Gaulle** is about 15 km (9 miles) from the Euro Disney Resort and 24 km (15 miles) north-east of Paris, and has two terminals (CDG 2 principally for Air France flights). **Orly** is about 35 km (21 miles) from the Euro Disney Resort and just 14 km (9 miles) south of Paris. Most intercontinental flights use Charles-de-Gaulle, a space-age modular construction. Both airports have banks for currency exchange, good restaurants, snack bars, post offices and duty-free shops.

Euro Disney shuttle buses *(navettes)* leave from Charles-de-Gaulle every 30 minutes from 8 a.m.–8 p.m., and from Orly every 45 minutes from 9 a.m.–7 p.m. (These times may vary outside high season.) The fare is 65 francs, with no reduction for children. The buses drop passengers at the RER station by the entrance to Euro Disneyland and at each of the six Euro Disney hotels. For Camp Davy Crockett, change at the RER station to the camp shuttle.

There is a regular and comfortable **public bus service** between the airports and from the airports to Paris. The buses leave at frequent intervals from about 6 a.m.–11 p.m. The Paris terminal *(aérogare)* for Charles-de-Gaulle airport is at Porte Maillot, near the Etoile; you can also board the bus at the Arc de Triomphe (avenue Carnot). Orly is served by the Invalides terminal. The average journey time from these terminals is about 40 minutes; it takes an hour and a quarter to get from one airport to the other by bus. Expect longer journey times during peak traffic hours.

To beat the traffic jams, there is also a cheap **rail service**. Trains leave every 15 minutes from about 5 a.m.–11 p.m. and take 45 minutes from Gare du Nord to Charles-de-Gaulle. A frequent all-day service from Musée d'Orsay, Saint-Michel or Austerlitz stations to Orly takes 40–60 minutes.

ANIMALS. Pets are not allowed inside Euro Disneyland or anywhere in the resort, but an **Animal Care Center** has been set up at the main car park (to the right of the moving walkway as you come in). There is space for nearly 300 dogs and cats. Bring your animal's papers. For a fee of 45 francs per day (65 francs extra overnight), your pet is fed and cared for. Euro Disney employees have had special training and look after the animals till 1 a.m.

BANKS and CURRENCY EXCHANGE OFFICES (*banque; bureau de change*). At Euro Disneyland there are two Banque Nationale de Paris **automatic cash tills** on Main Street – in Liberty Arcade and Discovery Arcade. **Currency exchange booths** are located at the Main Entrance and at the information booths at Main Street Station, Frontierland Depot, Adventureland and Fantasyland. Exchange facilities also exist at the hotels and the Festival Disney entertainment complex.

In Paris **banking hours** vary, but most banks open 9 a.m.–4.30 p.m., Mondays to Fridays. A few banks and currency exchange offices operate later and at weekends, especially those at the major railway stations and airports. The Paris Tourist Information Office (see p.124) can provide a full list. Carry your passport for all transactions.

I want to change some pounds/dollars.	**Je voudrais changer des livres sterling/dollars.**

BUS SERVICE. Free **shuttle buses** transport Euro Disney hotel guests to and from the RER station, by the theme park entrance, starting about one hour before the opening of the park and stopping one hour after closing. The half-hour trip to or from Camp Davy Crockett runs roughly every 12 minutes. The eight-minute trip from Newport Bay Club, Sequoia Lodge and Hotel New York runs every 6–15 minutes according to demand. The same applies to the shuttle serving Hotel Cheyenne and Hotel Santa Fe.

Paris buses (*autobus*) are not always fast, but they are a great way to see the town. Stops are marked by red and yellow signs, with bus numbers posted. Most buses run from 7 a.m.–8.30 p.m., some till midnight, in particular two serving RER stations for the Euro Disney Resort (63 for Gare de Lyon and 96 for Châtelet). There is a reduced service on Sundays and holidays. You use one or two tickets depending on the distance. You can buy a ticket on boarding the bus, but it's cheaper to buy a book (*carnet*) of 10 tickets at a Métro station or special one-, three- or five-day tourist passes, valid for Métro and/or bus journeys.

C **CAR HIRE** (*location de voitures*). At the Euro Disney Resort, car hire is available through Europcar, who have offices in the park and at the hotels. In Paris, this and other major companies offer both French and foreign makes of car. Local companies often charge lower rates, but they may set restrictive conditions, such as having to return the car to the same place.

You must produce a valid driving licence (held for at least one year) and your passport. Depending on the model you rent and the hiring firm, the minimum age for renting a car varies from 21–25. If you do not have a major credit card you must pay a substantial (refundable) deposit for the car.

CHILDREN. No problem at Euro Disneyland wondering what to do to keep them amused. But report **missing children** to the Lost Children office adjacent to the Plaza Gardens Restaurant, just off Main Street. Elsewhere in the park, the information booths can help, or telephone Guest Relations: 6474 3000.

A **Baby Care Center**, also next to the Plaza Gardens Restaurant, provides facilities for preparing baby food, warming bottles, breast-feeding and changing nappies. Disposable nappies and a small range of baby foods are on sale. You will also find facilities for changing nappies in the toilets. A few pushchairs (strollers) are available for rental at Town Square Terrace on Main Street, USA.

Gentle warning: Babies under one year old are not allowed aboard the Dumbo ride in Fantasyland, Orbitron and Autopia in Discoveryland, or Big Thunder in Frontierland.

Babysitting services are available at the Disney hotels and at the Festival Disney entertainment centre. Many Paris hotels provide a similar service or can help you locate reputable student and service organizations that provide babysitters (*garde d'enfant, babysitter*).

Can you get me a babysitter for tonight/tomorrow night?	**Pouvez-vous me trouver une baby-sitter pour ce soir/demain soir?**

CLOTHING. Although clothing at Euro Disneyland is naturally casual, you cannot go barefoot or bare-chested. Take a sweater for cool evenings or a light raincoat when the weather's uncertain, as it can be in the Paris region. The importance of good walking shoes cannot be overemphasized, both for Euro Disneyland and for your excursions to and 112 around Paris.

It may surprise you that the world's fashion capital is much more relaxed in its dress habits than many British or American cities. In the evening, casual or discreet elegance is often appreciated much more in Paris than formal wear, though nobody will object to you dressing up if you want to. Restaurants may require men to wear a jacket, but very rarely insist on a tie, and women are trusted to show their own good taste, whether in trousers or a dress.

COMPLAINTS (*réclamation*). On the rare occasion that something may go wrong at Euro Disneyland, report it to the City Hall on Main Street, USA, or telephone Guest Relations on 6474 3000.

In Paris, if you cannot get satisfaction at your hotel or restaurant, contact the Tourist Information Office (*office du tourisme*), tel. 4723 6172, where you should be able to get English-speaking help. Serious complaints may also be taken to the local police station (*commissariat de police*).

Bad merchandise: Within about ten days of purchase, a store will usually exchange faulty merchandise if you have the receipt, but you are more likely to be given a credit than to get your money back.

I'd like to make a complaint.   **J'ai une réclamation à faire.**

CONVERTER CHARTS. France uses the metric system.

Temperature

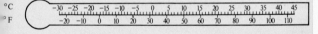

Length

cm

inches

metres

ft./yd.

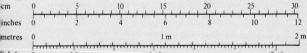

Weight

grams

ounces

C **CREDIT CARDS and TRAVELLER'S CHEQUES** (*carte de crédit; chèque de voyage, 'traveller's'*).

Credit cards. The major cards are accepted throughout the Euro Disney Resort. In Paris most hotels, restaurants, shops, car-hire firms and tourist-related businesses accept certain credit cards, especially the bank cards.

Traveller's cheques. Again, these are accepted almost everywhere (except at shops and restaurants inside the theme park) at the Euro Disney Resort, as well as **Eurocheques** and **personal cheques** drawn on French banks with passport identification. In Paris, hotels, travel agents and many shops accept them, although the exchange rate is invariably better at a bank.

Paying cash. Some shops or hotels may accept payment in sterling or dollars, but the exchange rate will not be as good.

Do you accept traveller's cheques?	**Acceptez-vous les chèques de voyage?**
Can I pay with this credit card?	**Puis-je payer avec cette carte de crédit?**

CRIME (*délit*). For all Euro Disney's efficient security service, some pickpockets and thieves are bound to try their luck, so watch your wallet or handbag, especially in crowds. Keep valuable items in your hotel safe and obtain a receipt for them.

Lock your car at all times and leave nothing valuable on view inside. Any loss or theft should be reported at once to your Disney hotel or to the Information Office at City Hall on Main Street, USA.

In Paris, contact the nearest *commissariat de police* (see POLICE).

I want to report a theft.	**Je veux signaler un vol.**
My ticket/wallet/passport/hand-bag/credit card has been stolen.	**On a volé mon billet/ portefeuille/passeport/ sac à main/(ma) carte de crédit.**

CURRENCY (*monnaie*). For currency restrictions, see CUSTOMS CONTROLS. The French franc (abbreviated F or FF) is divided into 100 centimes. Current coins include 5-, 10-, 20- and 50-centime pieces as well as 1-, 2-, 5- and 10-franc pieces. Banknotes come in denominations of 20, 50, 100, 200 and 500 francs.

Could you give me some (small) change? **Pouvez-vous me donner de la (petite) monnaie?**

CUSTOMS CONTROLS (*douane*). There's no limit on the importation or exportation of local or foreign currencies or traveller's cheques, but amounts exceeding 50,000 French francs or equivalent must be declared on arrival.

The following chart shows some main items you may take into France:

	Cigarettes	Cigars	Tobacco	Spirits	Wine
1)	400	100	500 g	1 l	2 l
2)	300 or	75 or	400 g	1 ½ l and	5 l
3)	200	50	250 g	1 l	2 l

1) Visitors arriving from outside Europe
2) Visitors arriving from EC countries with non-duty-free items
3) Visitors arriving from EC countries with duty-free items, or from other European countries

I've nothing to declare.	**Je n'ai rien à déclarer.**
It's for my own use.	**C'est pour mon usage personnel.**

DISABLED VISITORS. Euro Disneyland is splendidly user-friendly for disabled visitors. Every effort has been made to ensure that a maximum number of attractions is easily accessible. **Restrictions** are necessary at three rides – Frontierland's Big Thunder Mountain railroad and Discoveryland's Star Tours and Autopia. People with serious back or muscular problems are advised not to go on these.

The booklet, *Guest Special Services Guide*, which details special access to attractions, restaurants and shops, is available at City Hall on Main Street. Where visitors need special assistance in boarding some of the ride vehicles, they should have a companion with them, as Euro Disneyland employees do not have the necessary training. **Wheelchairs** can be rented inside the Main Entrance at Town Square Terrace.

Special Services Parking is located next to the Disneyland Hotel. For **sight-impaired** visitors, City Hall provides complimentary audio cassettes and portable tape players describing the attractions. **Guide dogs** are allowed at most of the park's attractions, restrictions being listed in the *Guest Special Services Guide*. City Hall also provides telephone devices for those with **impaired hearing**.

D **DRIVING IN FRANCE.** To take a car into France, you will need:

- A valid driving licence
- Car registration papers
- A red warning triangle and a spare set of bulbs

The green card is no longer obligatory, but full insurance coverage is strongly recommended.

Drivers and passengers, front and rear, are required by law to wear seat belts. Children under ten may not travel in the front (unless the car has no back seat). Driving on a provisional licence is not permitted in France. The minimum age is 18.

Driving regulations: As elsewhere on the Continent, drive on the right, overtake on the left, yield right-of-way to all vehicles coming from the right (except on roundabouts) unless otherwise indicated. Speed limits are 45 or 60 kph (28 or 37 mph) in residential areas, 90 kph (56 mph) on through roads, 110 kph (68 mph) on dual carriageways and 130 kph (81 mph) on motorways, called *autoroutes*. In fog, all highway speeds are limited to 60 kph (37 mph) and on wet roads all limits are reduced by 10 kph (6 mph). The word *rappel* means a restriction is continued.

Parking at Euro Disneyland. The visitors' car park has room for 11,500 cars. Each row of parking places is marked by a Disney character (Alice, Bambi, Jiminy Cricket, Pinocchio, etc.). Note this along with the number and letter of your parking place before taking the two-way moving walkway to the park entrance. There is a separate car park for disabled visitors next to the Disneyland Hotel.

Parking in Paris. This is a major problem. In the centre, practically all parking is metered. Use underground car parks for extended parking. Fines for violations are heavy and tow-aways are not uncommon.

Fuel and oil: Fuel is available in super (98 octane), normal (90 octane), lead free (but don't expect to find it at every village pump; 95 octane) and diesel. All grades of motor oils are on sale. Service-station attendants are tipped for any additional services rendered.

Fluid measures

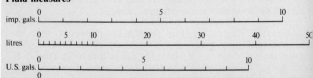

Distance

km 0   1   2   3   4   5   6   8   10   12   14   16
miles 0 ½ 1 1½ 2   3   4   5   6   7   8   9   10

Road signs: Most road signs are the standard pictographs used throughout Europe, but you may encounter these written signs as well:

Accotements non stabilisés	Soft shoulders
Chaussée déformée	Bad road surface
Déviation	Diversion
Douane	Customs
Gravillons	Loose gravel
Impasse	Cul-de-sac
Péage	Toll
Priorité a droit	Give way to traffic from right
Ralentir	Slow
Sauf riverains	Entry prohibited except for inhabitants of street
Sens unique	One-way street
Serrez à droite/gauche	Keep right/left
Sortie de camions	Lorry exit
Stationnement interdit	No parking
Véhicules lents	Slow vehicles

driving licence	**permis de conduire**
car registration papers	**carte grise**
Are we on the road to...?	**Sommes-nous sur la route de...?**
Fill the tank, please.	**Le plein, s'il vous plaît.**
normal/super/lead-free	**normale/super/sans plombe**

EMBASSIES and CONSULATES (*ambassade; consulat*). If your passport or money have been lost or stolen, if you have problems with the police or have suffered a serious accident, you will need to contact your embassy or consulate at the address below:

Australia	embassy and consulate, 4 rue jean-Rey, 75015 Paris; tel. 4059 3300.
Canada	embassy-chancellery, 35 avenue Montaigne, 75008 Paris; tel. 4723 0101.

E

Eire	embassy-chancellery, 12 avenue Foch (enter from 4 rue Rude), 75016 Paris; tel. 4500 2087.
New Zealand	embassy-chancellery, 7 ter rue Léonard-de-Vinci, 75016 Paris; tel. 4500 2411.
South Africa	embassy, 59 quai d'Orsay, 75007 Paris; tel. 455 9237.
United Kingdom	embassy, 35 rue du Faubourg Saint-Honoré, 75008 Paris; tel. 4266 9142 consulate, 16 rue d'Anjou, 75008 Paris (same telephone number).
USA	embassy-chancellery, 2 avenue Gabriel, 75008 Paris; tel. 4296 1202.

Where's the ... embassy/consulate? American/British Canadian/Irish	**Où se trouve l'ambassade/ le consulat ...? américaine/britannique canadienne/irlandaise**

EMERGENCIES (*urgence*). You can get assistance anywhere in France by dialling number 17 for the police (*Police-Secours*); 18 for the fire brigade (*pompiers*). For urgent medical problems outside Euro Disney, dial SOS Médecins: 4007 7777 or SAMU: tel. 4567 5050.

Inside Euro Disneyland, **First Aid** is available next to the Plaza Gardens Restaurant, Main Street, USA.

ENTRANCE. Tickets, known as Euro Disneyland Passports and Child Passports (for ages 3–11), may be bought at any Main Entrance ticket booth or at your Disney hotel information desk. They give unlimited access to all park shows and attractions – except the Rustler Roundup Shootin' Gallery (see pp.44–5). The prices listed below are correct at the time of going to press, but are subject to change without notice. Children under seven must be accompanied by an adult and those aged two and under are admitted free.

You can leave the park and return on the same day without extra payment if you get a re-entry stamp on your hand and keep your Euro Disneyland Passport.

	1-Day Passport	2-Day Passport	3-Day Passport
Child	150 F	285 F	375 F
Adult (over 11)	225 F	425 F	565 F

GUIDED TOURS. Official Euro Disneyland tour guides are on hand to take you on a walking tour, with extra information about the park and the Walt Disney Company. Purchase a Guided Tour ticket (in addition to your Euro Disneyland Passport) at the Main Entrance or City Hall on Town Square. For groups of 15 or more, advance reservations should be made through Guest Relations; tel. 6474 3000.

    Guests at the Disney hotels should inquire at the hotel information desk about excursions to Paris and other sights in the region (see pp.96–104).

G

HAIRDRESSERS (*coiffeur*). At the Euro Disney Resort men and women can have their hair done at the Hotel New York. Men can also go to the Harmony Barber Shop on Main Street, USA (see p.41). Otherwise, Paris is your best bet and there the choice is enormous.

H

I'd like a perm/blow-dry. **J'aimerais une permanente/ un brushing.**

HOTELS and ACCOMMODATION (*hôtel; logement*). For reservations at Euro Disney Resort hotels and Camp Davy Crockett, write to: Central Reservations Office, BP 105, 77777 Marne-la-Vallée Cedex 4, France; tel. (33 1) 4941 4910; fax (33 1) 4930 7100 and 4930 7170. Residents of the UK may also call (071) 753 2900 for information and reservations.

    If you are staying in Paris and have not booked accommodation in advance, there are information desks to help you at the airports and railway stations. The Paris Tourist Information Office (see p.124) offers a booklet listing hotels. Or try the recommendations in the Berlitz PARIS TRAVEL GUIDE.

LAUNDRY. All the Disney hotels and Camp Davy Crockett have coin-operated laundry facilities.

L

LOST PROPERTY (*objets trouvés*). Missing articles in the Euro Disney Resort can be reported or claimed at City Hall on Main Street, USA, tel. 6474 3000.

119

L

In Paris lost property is sent to the Bureau des Objets Trouvés, 36 rue des Morillons, 75015. Forms must be filled out in French, but there is usually an English-speaker there to help you. If you've lost your passport, check first with your embassy – that's where the Bureau des Objets Trouvés sends it.

I've lost my wallet/handbag/passport.	**J'ai perdu mon portefeuille/sac/passeport.**

M **MEDICAL CARE**. See also EMERGENCIES. Make sure your health insurance policy covers any illness or accident while on holiday.

Visitors from EC countries with corresponding health insurance facilities are entitled to medical and hospital treatment under the French social security system. Before leaving home, ensure that you have the appropriate forms required to obtain this benefit in case of need.

If you fall ill while staying at the Euro Disney Resort, first aid and infirmary facilities are on hand.

In the Paris area, two private hospitals serve the Anglo-American community: American Hospital of Paris, 63 bd. Victor-Hugo, 92202 Neuilly, tel. 4747 5300; Hôpital Franco-Britannique, 48 rue de Villiers, Levallois-Perret; tel. 4758 1312.

Chemists (*pharmacies*) with green crosses are helpful with minor ailments or finding a nurse (*infirmière*) if you need injections or other special care. The Pharmacie des Champs-Elysées, 84 avenue des Champs-Elysées, tel. 4562 0241, is open 24 hours a day.

I need a doctor/dentist.	**Il me faut un médecin/dentiste.**
I've a pain here.	**J'ai mal ici.**
an upset stomach	**mal à l'estomac**
a fever	**de la fièvre**
headache	**mal à la tête**

METRO. Ideal for linking up with the RER line out to the Euro Disney Resort, Paris's underground transport is perhaps the world's most efficient, fastest and cleanest. It's also cheaper than most. If you are planning a few trips, buy a cut-rate book of 10 tickets (*carnet*).

Which line should I take for ...?	**Quelle direction dois-je prendre pour ...?**

NEWSPAPERS and MAGAZINES. The *International Herald Tribune* and British newspapers are on sale at the newsstand in the Euro Disney RER station and in the Disney hotels. They are of course also available at kiosks all over Paris.

OPENING HOURS. Euro Disneyland is open 365 days a year. During high season the park opens in general from 9 a.m.–midnight, but all times are subject to change without notice, so check with Guest Relations; tel. 6474 3000. 'High season' is determined more or less by the French calendar of public and school holidays: i.e. Easter and the following two weeks; spring weekends; 1 May (*Fête du Travail*), 8 May (*Fête de la Libération*); summer (mid-June to early September); the week around 1 November, All Saints' Day (*Toussaint*), and the week from Christmas to New Year's Day. In the winter months outside Christmas week, the park is generally open 10 a.m.–6 p.m. The rest of the year, opening hours are 9 a.m.–7 p.m. or 9 p.m.

POLICE (*police*). An increasing number of the younger generation of Paris police officers speak English. In case of need, the number to dial is 17.

Where's the nearest police station? **Où est le commissariat de police le plus proche?**

POST OFFICES. You will find post boxes throughout the theme park. Mail is collected daily. There's a post office in the Festival Disney entertainment complex. In Paris, besides the neighbourhood offices advertised by the blue bird on a yellow background, there is also a 24-hour main post office at 52 rue du Louvre. In addition to the normal postal facilities, you can make local or long-distance telephone calls, send telegrams and receive or send money. Stamps may also be bought from tobacconists.

A stamp for this letter/postcard, please. **Un timbre pour cette lettre/carte postale, s'il vous plaît**

I want to send a telegram to ... **J'aimerais envoyer un télégramme à ...**

P **PUBLIC HOLIDAYS** (*jour férié*). Below are the French national holidays. Public offices and banks, as well as most shops, are closed. Euro Disneyland and the rest of the Euro Disney Resort, of course, remain open.

1 January	*Jour de l'An*	New Year's Day
1 May	*Fête du Travail*	Labour Day
8 May	*Fête de la Libération*	Victory Day (1945)
14 July	*Fête Nationale*	Bastille Day
15 August	*Assomption*	Assumption
1 November	*Toussaint*	All Saints' Day
11 November	*Anniversaire de l'Armistice*	Armistice Day
25 December	*Noël*	Christmas Day
Moveable dates	*Lundi de Pâques*	Easter Monday
	Ascension	Ascension
	Lundi de Pentecôte	Whit Monday

R **RADIO and TV** (*radio, télévision*). All the Disney hotel rooms have TVs, which show closed-circuit films and pick up international channels in addition to the seven French channels. Top-rated Paris hotels have similar facilities. On the radio you can pick up BBC World Service on 648 medium wave and BBC Radio 4 on 198 long wave.

S **SMOKING.** Smoking is forbidden inside Euro Disneyland attractions, but permitted in the open air and in designated areas of most restaurants. All Disney hotels have some designated non-smoking rooms.

Tobacco is a state monopoly in France, making foreign brands more expensive than French cigarettes – available with dark or light tobacco, with or without filter. Tobacco shops and tobacco counters in cafés, bars and many newsagents are advertised in the street by a conspicuous double red cone. Tobacco products are on sale at Festival Disney, near Champion's Sports Bar.

A packet of .../A box of matches, please.
filter-tipped/without filter
122 light/dark tobacco

**Un paquet de.../Une boîte d'allumettes, s'il vous plaît.
avec/sans filtre
du tabac blond/brun**

TAXIS. At the Euro Disney Resort a limited number of taxis will be stationed near the RER station. Otherwise, hotels can order you a taxi, but be warned that the meter starts running from the vehicle's point of departure, not from the moment of pick-up. In addition to the price indicated on the meter, there are charges for luggage, which should be listed inside the taxi.

TELEPHONE. All but the smallest hotels in France have direct dialling in each room. If you need help in placing a call, ask your hotel to do it or go to the post office.

Though they are still found in post offices, coin-operated phones are practically a thing of the past in the Paris area, replaced by the 'Télécarte' system. These phone cards can be bought (minimum price 40 francs) at post offices and from tobacconists. At the Euro Disney Resort, they are available at the RER station, the post office in Festival Disney, and various points around the theme park.

For calls abroad from France, dial 19 followed, after the change of tone, by the country's dialling code (UK 44, USA and Canada both 1), the area code and the subscriber's number. Remember for the UK to drop the first 0 in the area code.

TIME DIFFERENCES. France follows Greenwich Mean Time + 1, and in summer the clocks are put forward one hour.

Summer chart:

New York	London	**Paris**	Sydney	Auckland
6 a.m.	11 a.m.	**noon**	8 p.m.	10 p.m.

TIPPING (*pourboire*). A 15 per cent service charge is generally included automatically in hotel and restaurant bills. In Paris, as at the Eurodisney Resort, rounding off the overall bill is an accepted friendly gesture to the waiter. It is also customary to give porters, doormen, petrol station attendants, etc., a coin or two for their service.

T **TOILETS** (*toilettes*). The Euro Disney Resort has very high standards of hygiene and has provided plenty of toilet facilities throughout the theme park.

In Paris, your best bets in public are the WCs in cafés. They are usually free, but it is courteous to order at least a coffee. In restaurants or hotels, a saucer with small change in it is the sign that a tip is expected. If the toilet has no apparent light switch, the light will go on when you lock the door.

TOURIST INFORMATION OFFICE (*office du tourisme*). Paris's main office is very efficient: 127 avenue des Champs-Elysées, 75008 Paris; tel. 4723 6172. Other branches are located in the main railway stations, airports and the terminals at the Invalides and Porte Maillot, and in Festival Disney.

TRAINS. The French National Railways (*Société des Chemins de Fer Français* or SNCF) run fast, punctual and comfortable trains, of which the best are the high-speed TGV, due to stop directly at Euro Disney in 1994.

In Paris, among the main stations are Gare du Nord (for British connections) and Gare de Lyon for the RER train out to Euro Disney at Marne-la-Vallée.

W **WATER** (*eau*). Tap water is safe in the Paris region, except when marked *eau non potable* (not for drinking). Carbonated and still mineral waters are available everywhere.

a bottle of mineral water	**une bouteille d'eau minérale**
fizzy/still	**gazeuse/non gazeuse**

SOME USEFUL EXPRESSIONS

yes/no	**oui/non**
please/thank you	**s'il vous plaît/merci**
excuse me	**excusez-moi**
you're welcome	**je vous en prie**
where/when/how	**où/quand/comment**

EXPRESSIONS

how long/how far	**combien de temps/à quelle distance**
yesterday/today/tomorrow	**hier/aujourd'hui/demain**
day/week/month/year	**jour/semaine/mois/année**
left/right	**gauche/droit**
up/down	**en haut/en bas**
good/bad	**bon/mauvais**
big/small	**grand/petit**
cheap/expensive	**bon marché/cher**
hot/cold	**chaud/froid**
old/new	**vieux/neuf**
open/closed	**ouvert/fermé**
Where are the toilets?	**Où sont les toilettes?**
Does anyone here speak English?	**Y a-t-il quelqu'un ici qui parle anglais?**
I don't understand.	**Je ne comprends pas.**
Please write it down.	**Veuillez bien me l'écrire.**
What does this mean?	**Que signifie ceci?**
Waiter/Waitress!	**S'il vous plaît!**
Help me, please.	**Aidez-moi, s'il vous plaît.**
Get a doctor – quickly!	**Un médecin, vite!**
What time is it?	**Quelle heure est-il?**
I'd like ...	**J'aimerais ...**
How much is that?	**C'est combien?**

DAYS OF THE WEEK

Sunday	**dimanche**	Thursday	**jeudi**
Monday	**lundi**	Friday	**vendredi**
Tuesday	**mardi**	Saturday	**samedi**
Wednesday	**mercredi**		

INDEX

For index to Practical Information, see inside front cover.

029/206 RP